From Where Life Flows: The Local Knowledge
and Politics of Water in the Andes

From Where Life Flows: The Local Knowledge and Politics of Water in the Andes

Editors: Frode F. Jacobsen & John-Andrew McNeish

tapir academic press

© Tapir Academic Press, Trondheim 2006

ISBN   82-519-2144-9
ISBN 13 978-82-519-2144-2

This publication may not be reproduced, stored in a retrieval system or transmitted in any form or by any means; electronic, electrostatic, magnetic tape, mechanical, photo-copying, recording or otherwise, without permission.

Layout: PDC Tangen AS
Cover layout: Tapir Academic Press
Printed by Tapir Uttrykk
Binding: Grafisk Produksjonsservice AS
Paper: 90g G-print

Tapir Academic Press
N–7005 TRONDHEIM
Tel.:   + 47 73 59 32 10
Fax: + 47 73 59 32 04
E-mail: forlag@tapir.no
www.tapirforlag.no

Contents

Local Water Management Stategies in the Andes and Beyond 7
   John Andrew McNeish & Frode Jacobsen

Part I 35
Introduction Part I: Albarradas in Coastal Ecuador: Rescuing Traditional
Knowledge on Sustainable Use of Biodiversity 35
   Jorge G. Marcos
Water Management in Ancient Ecuador 41
   Jorge G. Marcos
The Use and Traditional Knowledge of Pre-Hispanic Hydraulic Systems amongst
Indigenous and Non-Indigenous Populations on the Ecuadorian Coast 53
   Silvia G. Álvarez
The Future of the Albarradas: Between Local Knowledge and «Development» Policies 64
   Claudia Gonzalez Andricaín
Two Stories about Development on the Peninsula Santa Elena, Ecuador 75
   Frode F. Jacobsen

Part II 87
Introduction Part II: Bolivia: The Politics of Water 87
   John-Andrew McNeish
Establishing Development Orthodoxy: Negotiating Masculinities in the Water Sector . 91
   Nina Laurie
Managing Scarcity of Water: Notes about Political Mobilisations in Poor
Neighbourhoods of El Alto, Bolivia 113
   Franck Poupeau
Irrigation: When the Solution became a Problem 126
   Pablo Regalsky

Part III 137
Local Level Water Management and the Progress of Civilizations in the Ancient
Near East: A comparative case 137
   Oystein La Bianca
Presentation of authors 151

Acknowledgements

We thank the Norwegian Research Council and the International Office at the University of Bergen for their generous support of the Local Knowledge and Natural Resource Management network. Their support has allowed us to hold several workshops in Europe and Latin America, the first published result of which is this book. We are also grateful to the Centre for Environmental and Resource Studies (SMR), now part of Department of biology, University of Bergen, and the Centre for Development Studies (CDS) for their logistical and intellectual support. Finally, we thank Professor Penny Harvey of the Department of Anthropology, University of Manchester, UK for her thorough and constructive work as our external reader.

The editors

Local Water Management Stategies in the Andes and Beyond

John Andrew McNeish & Frode Jacobsen

Introduction: More than Water

For anyone aware of recent events in the Andean region it will be obvious not only how important water and other natural resources are, but the degree to which they remain a central issue of social demand and political conflict. Indeed, this is true not only in the Andean region, but throughout many regions of the world where such resources are scarce due to local climate, or because of their exclusion by ownership and cost from the majority of the populace. In the countries of the Andean Cordillera a reliance on a temperamental weather system, coupled with a history of over-exploitation and growing climate change has made water not only a scarce commodity, but a vital part of both local politics and cosmology.

For Andean peoples water is much more than a hydratic resource, it is a living being and the provider of life and animation for the universe. Whilst there are local differences, in the dominant indigenous cultures of the region, Aymara and Quechua societies, water flows from *Wirakocha*, the creator god of the universe who fertilizes the earth and permits the reproduction of life. Each year during the rainy season in the Bolivian Highlands the local ceremony *yaku cambio* (the change of waters) symbolizes the centrality of water as a unifying force. In this ceremony local people collect together water from all the wells, rivers and streams in their community territory in an effort to bind together the regenerative forces of their political and natural environment (Sikkink 1997, McNeish 2001).

Treasured as the source of life and well-being, Andean peoples have developed differing techniques and customs to conserve and manage water and to use this to create and sustain cultivable lands. Urban life and commercial development have in many incidences removed or transformed these techniques, but it is quite clear from current politics and agricultural practice that there continues to be a great concern with and a deep well of knowledge about water conservation and management.

Although the cosmological side to water lies beyond our scope, in this book we aim to study some of the content of this knowledge and to study the existing techniques used by Andean peoples to manage and conserve their water supplies. The book not only demonstrates the incredible history and appropriateness of such technology to distinct local environments, but argues that given the current politics of water in the region, efforts should be made to both conserve and consider the further development and spread of this know-how and methods. We furthermore argue that such know-how and methods are important tools of survival in a region of high and rising poverty.

In taking account of these different qualities of water the book aims not only to be multi-disciplinary in its formation, but to also highlight that a comprehensive understanding of the importance of this natural resource requires consideration of its multi-dimensional character as a natural, economic, political and cultural force. In this introductory chapter we run through the background to which the following chapters belong and will highlight the wider complexity and difficulty of this multi-dimensional character.

A Perspective on Local Knowledge

It is widely acknowledged that social studies of practices where people employ their local knowledge in activities of daily life are much needed because they throw light on the 'social construction of knowledge' as an important dimension of both everyday practices and scientific discourses. Such studies highlight the practical priorities that local people make in their daily lives, and are hence considered in the development literature as a necessary step in achieving local participation in projects for change (Chambers 1994, Martinez 1996; Mohan 1996; Webster 2002). This book aims to make this step, but by adopting a multi-disciplinary approach that emphasises the way in which social practice is tied to wider contemporary and historical (as well as archaeological) practices and events, we further aim to create a theoretical basis that is broader than earlier studies that used such labels as indigenous knowledge. In doing so we also aim to form a more critical perspective of what is understood as being indigenous knowledge, as well as its capacities and limitations.

The research tradition on indigenous knowledge is fraught with potential pitfalls. Contributions to this tradition have frequently led to a reification of local dynamic ways of resource management. In earlier anthropological writing, indigenous knowledge has frequently been viewed as something that necessarily contributed to sustainable resource management (Ellen et al. 2000). However, this idealised picture of indigenous knowledge and practice is becoming increasingly questioned. The anthropological tradition focusing on indigenous knowledge continues to enhance our understanding of alternative knowledge traditions and to help justify the authority and standing of such traditions, in relation to state as well as non-government organisations. However, more recent writing argues that the essentialisation and romantisation of an asserted original folk knowledge (e.g. within the field of conflict management) are often tools employed by politicians representing a so-called indigenous population for furthering particular political aims in the present (see for example, Sieder & Witchell 2001). With an increasing awareness of the effects of migration and globalisation, it has also become clear to anthropologists that these kinds of knowledges and practices can no longer be seen as restricted to indigenous peoples, understood as existing in an isolated or static sense.

As a result of these problems with «indigenous knowledge» this book aims to further develop an understanding of 'local knowledge.' In this way we aim to avoid the inherent dangers of overlooking the valuable practical knowledge of people who don't define themselves strictly as indigenous, and in the case of people who conceive of themselves as indigenous, the risk of failing to detect present and past influences from outside the native communities on their knowledge. The latter may lead to a lack of insight into the dynamics and flexibility of local traditions. Local traditions may well have survived precisely because they are changing, and able to adapt to changes in the environment, culture and society (Bloch 1986). Several studies of local knowledge have been inspired by linguistic models and theories (D'Andrade 1995; Ellen 1993). Within the field of cognitive anthropology, an increasing number of anthropologists call for a greater stress on practical knowledge rather than primarily dealing with verbalized and verbalizable knowledge. As such, it has been argued that there is a need for more 'taskonomy' at the expense of 'taxonomy' (Dougherty & Keller 1982).

A focus on taskonomy requires a focus on the practical problems local people try to solve and the practical tasks they perform in doing so. It requires a consideration of both the verbal and tacit manner in which they order their tools, materials, work planning, work division and more. It implies investigating and mapping the systematization that people do without being conscious about creating a system. As in the logical, but tacit classification system that can be detected from studying how e.g. Californian blacksmiths are placing their equipment in a beautifully organized and routine way in a three-dimensional space (ibid.), ingenious systems of tacit classification may be spelled out from studies of water harvesting practices. This does not mean, however, that more abstractly formulated knowledge, outside particular work operations, cannot be studied. Rather, by focusing on real life events like quarrels, discussions and the clash of interests influencing practical issues of importance to local people, it is possible to study the outward expression of tacit knowledge (Goffman 1962). In this way one may also ensure that the researchers' attempts at mapping local knowledge will have relevance for the lives and priorities of the people studied.

By stressing local knowledge as embedded in the practical situations and concerns of local people, it is possible to avoid the reification of the concepts of knowledge and culture. Knowledge (and culture) as common understandings that are «more or less shared by members of a society» (Keesing 1975), but which also differentially influenced by factors such as gender, employment, socio-economic differences, age and locality. Part of this uneven distribution of knowledge relates to structures of power. Furthermore, instead of looking for a 'harmonic' or internally consistent systems or neat 'packages' of knowledge, researchers must also recognise that whilst certain knowledges may contain levels of abstraction, they may still function well for a multitude of different tasks and practical problems (Strauss 1997; Jacobsen 1998). One may also be able to map knowledge which 'works' for people without necessarily being part of the central cultural beliefs and convictions of each and every individual, and recognising instead that these beliefs are the product of a 'sociology of knowledge' (Spiro 1986).

Local knowledge, Local Priorities and Development

In recent years many international development organisations have been involved in funding research projects designed to further study, catalogue and find place for different kinds of local knowledge within development planning and policy (Korovkin 1998, Goldin 1996, Smith 1984). This work has been carried out on the basis of a recognition for the need for local participation in development planning and the value of existing techniques. This research has not, however, been related close enough with the preoccupations of those interested in the practical business of fighting poverty (Eversole, Ridgeway & Mercer 2004). Whilst aiming to highlight the importance of understanding local knowledge as a complex of competing relations, an important aim of this book is to argue that, given the clear value of local knowledge and practices of indigenous and other local peoples, this is clearly a mistake. Despite some interest in better engagement with local populations and their knowledge of the local environment, international development professionals and governments remain by and large focused on the development of anti-poverty programmes initiated, or at least funded by outsiders. As a result local people's own initiatives and strategies have remained largely invisible, except in cases where they can easily be capitalised on within existing external industries and markets e.g. bio-technology, organic products, crafts etc.

This book aims to offer a closer look at 'insider' or community-driven anti-poverty strategies. In our case this means focusing on local flexible strategies for securing water resources under demanding climatic conditions and during environmental changes. The research described here aims to identify the range of initiatives that have been created by and for members of indigenous communities to address such challenges, such as traditional structures for collecting run-off and rainwater (e.g 'atajadas' or detention ponds). The papers here further question how these strategies have been formed and made to operate. They also pose questions such as: What positive and negative lessons can be learned from the interplay between local knowledge and strategies and influx of knowledge and initiatives from the outside? How does this interplay impact on poverty reduction?

Although water harvesting methods and technologies, such as the *atajadas,* are labelled here as 'traditional' systems, we do not want to convey that these systems have remained unchanged over time. The use of the term 'traditional' here is intended to point to the fact that they have a long history, but also form part of human adaptation to the natural environment. This adaptation represents a co-evolutionary process that began when the first hunter gatherers started modifying the landscape. Later, in the Pre-Colombian neo-lithic of ancient coastal Ecuador, various ingenious water harvesting devises were adapted to the natural environment of the coastal landscape and to its climatic variation (see Marcos, this volume). In the flood plains raised fields, or so-called *camellones,* were developed, and on the hilltops water harvesting from local cloud-forests took place. In the semi-arid environment between these zones, a type of detention pond, *Jagüeyes* or *Albarradas,* was created where the permeable calciferous sediments of ancients raised shores provided a medium for the collection of artificial groundwater in an area mostly devoid of natural ground water. Of all these systems, only these detention ponds have survived and continue in use. However, their use has changed throughout history, being linked to cattle breeding after the Spanish colonization, and in the latest decades, used as a source of the clay used in building bricks. This flexible use of traditional water harvesting technologies can then be understood to be an age-old and successful locally driven survival strategy in several semi-arid areas from Southern California throughout Meso-America to Northern Peru.

Local priorities and international development

Given the emphasis on the importance of local people driving their own anti-poverty agendas, the dearth of practical studies on this topic is surprising (Eversole 2005). There is some work in the area of indigenous political movements and self-advocacy (e.g. Burgete Cal y Mayor 2000, Ramos 1998, Smith 1984) as well as a handful of studies dealing specifically with indigenous economic development (McBride 2001, Anderson 1997, Cornell and Kalt 1992) or 'ethno-development' in Latin America (Healy 2001, Partridge and Urquillas 1996). There is also a strong tradition of work in anthropology, and particularly economic anthropology, explicating the functioning and logic of non-Western social and economic systems, and following on this, some work has also been done on the changing economic strategies of indigenous peoples within their larger social and economic contexts (e.g. Korovkin 1998, Goldin 1996, Smith 1984). More recently Eversole, McNeish & Cimadamore (2005) have published a work proposing to study indigenous disadvantage worldwide and consider the difficult questions facing indigenous populations e.g the balance between autonomy and participation, the tensions underlying pro-poor and inclusionary development policies and the new spaces such policies create for indigenous peoples to advance their demands.

As these works make clear, the demands and priorities of indigenous and other local populations is a task fraught with several pitfalls. The expressed aim of many NGOs worldwide is to «empower» local communities through the introduction of participatory development. However, as several authors have recently argued, the concept of empowerment and its various uses by international, governmental and non-governmental organizations should be rigorously examined (Eversole, McNeish & Cimadamore 2005; Hickey & Mohan 2004). Whilst pro-poor pedagogues such as Paolo Freire linked participation to the betterment of unprivileged groups, participation in development and political representation, express an understanding of participatory development as the external improvement of individual opportunity in the international market economy (James 1999). Although the participatory methodologies of these organizations involve surveys of local priorities, frequently the final decision on priority areas for development are limited by the checks and balances put in place by external interests (McNeish 2001; also Gonzales Andricaín in this volume).

Participatory development, in which local priorities and local knowledge are the ostensible focus, may as a result not function as a suitable pro-poor strategy. The very concepts of local participation, local priorities and local knowledge and the way external actors like NGOs employ these concepts have to be scrutinized at the local level in order to uncover the real intent of external intervention. With these observations in mind a non-reifying approach focusing on the practical and flexible know-how of local actors in solving practical problems such as water harvesting is desirable. Such an approach requires researchers to not only listen carefully to what local people say, but to also give the local population a voice by learning from local people's everyday practice and application of traditional knowledge.

According to Posey (2000:189–90) there are numerous categories of traditional knowledge in local communities «which clearly have great potential for application in a wide range of sustainability strategies». Local populations conserve biological diversity, and in some cases provide other environmental benefits through, for example soil and water conservation, soil fertility enhancement, the management of game fisheries and forest management. By planting 'forest gardens' and managing the regeneration of bush fallows in ways that take advantage of natural processes and mimic the bio-diversity of natural forests, the natives of the Amazon offer a valuable route for using resources within the land's carrying capacity. The same can be said of much of the world's crop diversity, which is in the custody of farmers who follow-up age-old farming and land use practices that conserve bio-diversity and provide other benefits (Posey 2000: 189). Urban agriculture is an interesting and relatively new trend in this regard, where crop diversity and use of natural fertilizers typical of rural land use is 'transplanted' to towns (Cruz & Medina 2003, Egziabher et al. 1994, Mougeot 1994, Smit et al. 1996). The same may apply to traditional water harvesting systems, and to certain aspects of traditional water harvesting technologies.

Whilst there has been some discussion within academic circles of the possible contribution of indigenous ideas to sustainable development, or ethno-economics, the practical agents of development have, however, done little more than show their appreciation of the aesthetic, practical environmental and simple technical prowess of indigenous peoples. Although indigenous and local peoples are equally systematic in their means of gathering and categorising knowledge, the philosophical implications of economic systems that are based on personal relations, and not the accumulative rationale basis of market economics remain marginalised from dominant discourses. In this book we argue that without questioning the basis of the international economy in contrast to indigenous economic systems, the construction of its ethical and political structure remains beyond question, leaving the way open for abuse of indigenous and other local cultures.

The Formation of Knowledge

We argue here in line with other social and environmental scientists (Cavalcanti 2002) that an ontological shift encompassing different economic rationales is necessary. It has been demonstrated that whilst conventional western economics deals with the theory of goods, with its focus on the subjective relationship between consumers and objects of desire, other kinds of economics (of so-called exotic societies), refer to the 'personal relations' between people that the exchange of things (gifts) or labour (see Regalsky this volume) in certain social contexts creates (Gregory 1982: 8, Marshall 1976, Parry 1986, Weiner 1988, Wiessner 1981). A position that supports what Parry & Bloch (1989) label «long term cycles». The outcome of a model of society as an adjunct to the market is that, as Polanyi (1944:57) so well demonstrated, instead of the economy being embedded in social relations, 'social relations' are embedded in the economic system. National governments still appear incapable of relating to indigenous conceptions of development and poverty, or of the strongly related issues of the politics of rights and inclusion. It is worth underlining the fact that indigenous strategies for poverty reduction tie together environmental, social, economic and political issues (Eversole, Ridgeway & Mercer 2003).

Sufficient recognition of the way in which indigenous peoples constitute their knowledge of the environment, or of the way in which they manage it still lacks influence at the level of international development bureaucracy. Studies of ecological knowledge demonstrate that, as a matter of fact, it does not exist as a separate entity. It is not restricted to a simple compilation of data (Ellen *et al.* 2000, Posey 2000: 188). It exists as an element of the totality of the individual's bonds to the land and all living things, and as a part of the logically unified order of humankind, other beings and nature,[1] which also has a spiritual and super-natural dimension (Cavalcanti 2002; Marcos et al. 2004).

Knowledge among the natives of the Amazon of several aspects of the ecosystem such as medicinal plants, animal behaviour, climatic seasonality and forest and savannah management attests to a diversity of knowledge 'that can contribute to new strategies for ecologically and socially sound development' (Posey 2002). This does not happen by accident. It is the outcome of a long learning process that involves an accumulation of information through methods that are not necessarily informal and random. Quite the contrary, for an understanding of nature to make sense and to offer results, it is necessary that the natives classify, order and systematize the data that daily experience gives them.

Contrary to simple preconceptions this ordering has a physical impact on the local environment as well as human relations with it. As Posey demonstrated 'Many so-called «pristine» landscapes are in fact a *cultural landscape*, either create by humans or modified by human activity (such as natural forest management, cultivation and the use of fire). Too often environmental organizations aim at imposing 'natural states' on environments that in fact have a long history of modification by human activities, nurtured as such organizations may be by ideologies contrasting 'nature' with 'society' (Campbell 2005). Indigenous and other local populations, together with a growing number of analysts, believe that it is no longer acceptable simply to assume that just because landscapes and species appear to outsiders to be «natural» they are therefore «wild» (Cavalcanti 2002:48). Indeed, Fairchild and Leach (1998) have demonstrated how simplistic arguments supporting the notion of a pristine environmental past have and do threaten local populations. Fairchild and Leach demonstrate how colonial historians, botanists and social scientists colluded with each other to recreate Africa's environmental past. In this process idealistic European presumptions about a pristine pre-colonial environment in Africa were used to form the basis of a thesis of blame for environmental degradation that supported existing social prejudices and practices of colonial governance. The image created was of a forest covered zone that once housed only sparse hunter-gatherer or minimal root crop cultivator populations with a benign impact on forest cover (2000: 180). Colonial stereotypes concerning ethnicity were

---

1. «Nature» is of course a concept which content never is to be taken for granted. In any given society nature is culturally and socially constructed, and the way that nature relate to concepts like culture, may vary considerably cross-culturally (see e.g. Strathern 1980).

therefore linked to forest related practices, and forest loss could serve, in a mutually supportive way to reinforce ideas of ethnicity that marked out nomadic, or pastoral peoples as a danger to progress and development. In a similar vein, as demonstrated by Jacobsen in this volume, colonial imaginaries have been used and are still used to stigmatize local knowledge, technology and management systems in both Africa and the Andean region.

Fairchild and Leach (2000) show this thesis of forest lost due to demographic change was largely based on a mistaken reading of environmental history. New archeological and historical research from Ghana and the Ivory Coast shows there to have been much less forest cover in the past than assumed by colonial historians. Drawing together evidence from both these countries Fairchild and Leach calculate that deforestation during the 20th century has been significantly exaggerated across a large part of West Africa.

Exaggerated claims of deforestation have misled ecologists. Such claims have obscured the fact that present forest ecology and composition may reflect less «nature and its degradation» than real histories of climatic fluctuations in interaction with past land management. They may also obscure how migrant farmers may have enriched and managed their landscapes in sustainable ways. However, although mistaken, this thesis was to have a lasting impact on colonial policy as well as later development policy in the region and beyond. Indeed, with shifting cultivation usually seen as the key proximate cause, today's social science analyses of deforestation continues to highlight issues such as immigration into forest areas, technological change, poverty, tenure insecurity and population growth.

Water Technologies and Conflict

As well as describing the function and social significance of water harvesting systems, a further aim of this book is to highlight the wider political and economic context of local knowledge, and in particular knowledge about water harvesting. Water harvesting and irrigation systems form an important part of the vast knowledge that indigenous and local populations have of their natural environment. Such knowledge is embedded within complex social organisations, and forms the basis of both formal and important non-formal social networks. Indeed, together with the management of land, the management of water resources frequently provides the basis of social institutions and relationships on which ideas of belonging and community membership are tied (Marcos et al. 2004). For this reason it not surprising that ingenious large-scale and small-scale traditional water harvesting systems and their way of functioning have been documented by researchers in a range of societies in Latin-America, Asia and Africa (see e.g. Babiker 1996, Bicker et al. 2004, Bøe 2002, Pradhan & Gautam 2002; Varisco 1982,).

It may well be argued that their survival over thousands of years demonstrates the value of these systems in terms of effectiveness and flexibility. However, whilst such systems can be found in many parts of the world, researchers also identify many of these systems as under threat or as already abandoned, as several of the systems described from the Middle East by LaBianca (this volume) in fact are. Because of their long histories the reasons for this abandonment are not always easy to describe or explain. This said, it is likely that the movement of peoples and technological innovation have made some systems defunct.

Some correlation between the loss of traditional technology and the establishment of nation-states and expansion of public works and infrastructure can also be made. In many cases, as in Europe, this process was undoubtedly consensual and whilst marking the end of some technologies and social institutions also brought the advantages of new technology in terms of cleaner water supplies, as well as creating the basis of new social institutions. However, as La Bianca moreover demonstrates, local water harvesting systems have co-existed for centuries with the large-scale systems created as a result of development of states and empires in the Middle East. Their threat and abandonment cannot simply be expressed in terms of loss. However, the modern histories of many locations around the world reveal that the threat and abandonment of these systems have and can occur because of conflicts over natural resource ownership and the direct imposition by the state, or international system, of new technologies and logics of management and control.

Processes of stigmatization of poor peasant populations (native or not), and cultivation practices may also have contributed to the abandonment of traditional technologies (see Alvarez and Gonzales Andricaín in this volume). Furthermore, the preferences of NGOs and other external agents have also led to technical and functional changes in traditional water harvesting systems that make them less viable and more prone to abandonment (Jacobsen in this volume). As Swartley (2002: 156) has previously argued « the creating of any economic development project based on representations of the past, inherently calls for a critical understanding of the role of contemporary forces in framing these interpretations of the past».

Water has been a subject of conflict throughout history. Indeed, in modern development history it is perhaps surprising how much contention has been generated by competing interests for the ownership and control of water supplies. In recent history the best known of these conflicts have been the result of attempts by governments and the international community to build large-scale dam projects. The dam-building era for most of the rich countries of the North peaked during the middle decades of the last century (Usher 1997). By the 1970s, public opposition was such that industrial countries such as the United States, Norway, Sweden, Canada, Australia, France and Austria found themselves forced to look for new markets for dams. A building spree in the Third World resulted, aided by both bilateral and multilateral development aid institutions such as the World Bank. With their mandate to alleviate poverty, Western donors began to give dams as aid, in the name of bringing development and progress to the South. The bilateral agencies tended to channel this aid through their national dam-building companies, for which aid subsidies created competitive advantage in international bids.

The electricity and water reservoirs created material advantages for the countries where they were built, but the dams also resulted in the displacement of millions of people, decimated indigenous communities, drowned farmland and rainforest and devastated fisheries. Whilst the benefits of these projects helped to boost GNPs, the costs were mostly neglected and, until recent media coverage and legal cases, the impacts remained largely invisible (Usher 1997). Those most affected by aid financed dams tended to be marginalised groups such as peasants, tribal communities and landless people. Because of state repression and an unwillingness by the international community to accept criticism of efforts to help, for many years opposition to dam projects remained local and isolated. However, since the 1980s international opposition to large dam projects has gained in strength and breadth, largely due to the support of international environmental and human rights organisations. As a result of the overwhelming resistance to dams, the environmental and social impacts of such projects have become widely recognised. The World Bank no longer denies that dams can have potentially serious impacts and has tightened up its evaluation of potential environmental and social costs before giving support to such projects.

As a result of an increasing awareness of their possible damage, large-scale dam projects are no longer as fashionable symbols of development and modernisation as they once were. However, this change in fortunes does not mean that large-scale water projects, and projects involving foreign capital and technology have stopped (see e.g. Laurie 2005; Laurie et al. 2002). Indeed, as a result of this, nor does it mean that conflicts and reports of the environmental and social damage of such projects have stopped. Campaigns and protests in opposition to large-scale water projects and the privatisation of local water supplies continue to mark the local and national politics of most Latin American countries[2]. Ironically, despite their policies, this is also a problem that the international donor community are well aware of. In 1995 the vice president of the World Bank declared, «If the wars of this century were fought over oil, the wars of the next century will be fought over water.»

In a period of post-structural adjustment where targets for development and poverty reduction must be measurable and met, improved indicators, such as new water and sewerage connections have taken on a great political importance. Indeed, the water business is proving to be highly lucrative. The private for-profit water industry has grown explosively over the past decade. In 1990, private water companies operated in 12 countries; today they are in nearly 100. Industry analysts expect the private drinking water market to grow from its current level of about $500 billion to about $3 trillion in just the next five years (Barlow and Clarke 2002). The corporations typically sign long-term (25 to 30 year) contracts with a municipal or regional water authority that cedes to the corporation complete control over the water supply in question. The company sets rates and makes all investment decisions. Many contracts guarantee the private provider a minimum rate of return on investment, regardless of the quality of service. These contracts transfer control over a local or regional water supply to a single private company that is much more accountable to its shareholders than it is to any public entity or to water consumers.

As the water industry has become increasingly globalised, templates for privatisation have also been exported. The World Water Council is a policy-making think-tank, the membership role of which includes the World Bank, the UN, governments and the International Private Water Association. In 2000 at the Hague it recommended privatisation as a response to the global water crisis and successfully pushed the Council to endorse a for-profit principle: water is not a basic human right, but a commodity best

---

2. See Rio Hondo, Guatemala; Aguas Argentinas, Buenos Aires; Aguas de Tunari and Aguas de Illimani, Bolivia; Mato Grosso do Sol, Brazil; Aguas de Cartegena, Colombia; CONAIE Ecuador etc.

delivered by the private sector (Seabrook 2003). Despite the new poverty reduction discourse of the international development community, the local perception of efforts to improve water supplies through privatisation has been of a loss of ownership over natural resources.

In Bolivia the privatisation of water supplies in La Paz and Cochabamba, and the introduction of new technologies resulted in a series of demonstrations and campaigns to regain local control over local reservoirs and distribution. Although not directly linked in time to the series of demonstrations over the sale and ownership of oil and gas reserves in the country that resulted in the removal of the Sanchez de Losada administration in October 2004, the conflicts over water supplies involve the same social groups and echo much the same politics of mistrust in the state, desire for increased participation and citizenship (McNeish 2006). In the recent «water wars» in Cochabamba and La Paz, water users have demanded rights to greater involvement in government water management policies and to influence the regulation of the private water companies, Aguas de Tunari and Aguas de Illimani (Marvin & Laurie 1999). The protesters, representing a broad spectrum of urban and rural interests call for greater representation in company decisions over the level of service provision, the type and location of new connections and participation in debates about the concession's boundaries and duration.

Although the social character of these protests are particular to the historical and political context of Bolivia, these demands for renewed local controls have also been echoed in campaigns and protests in other parts of the continent. Indeed, the Ecuadorian government's privatisation of natural resources including water have resulted in a series of protests that are highly similar in their politically destabilising effects and calls for the recognition of local collective rights.

Alternative Management Strategies

As well as conflicts over the ownership and management of water resources, the experiences of privatisation have also created a heated debate over the goals, application and management of appropriate technologies. Following debates about the cost of water, an important concern within water service development is how economically accessible household connections are for the poor (Nickson 2001). As a result, attention is focused on technical innovation in order to discover other ways of delivering acceptable levels of service. Proposed solutions include shared connections, shallow averages, roof tanks and on-site sanitation (Water and Sanitation Programme 2001). Types of innovations vary and include non-conventional networks, such as condominial systems and technologies that reduce costs and payments like smart cards that allow pre-payment for water.

Demand side policies such as micro credit, community involvement and flexible water rates often complement and reinforce these supply-side improvements in order to make them more accessible (Brook & Tynan 1999). These schemes enable the costs of metering and secondary piping linkages to be covered as well as house connections. Alliances between private operators, the consumer, the State and NGOs are established with the aim of helping to make new connections more viable (Tynan 2000). In some cases pro-poor approaches recommend the flexibilisation of water quality standards in order to avoid imposing high, rigid, universal principles that are costly and discourage competition (Smith 2000; Brook & Tynan 1999).

Whilst in many cases these innovations have been successful in improving the coverage and quality of water supplies, this has not always been the case, as amply demonstrated by Poupeau in this volume. Indeed, as well as removing the options people once had in terms of choosing their supply, in some cases the privatisation of water supplies and the application of pro-poor technologies have resulted in the pollution of drinking water and the creation of other social impacts. For example, a recent report on the impact of the privatisation of the water supply in El Alto, the satellite city to Bolivian capital La Paz indicates that the kinds of pro-poor connections introduced were inappropriate to the physical and social formation of the community (Geoforum 2005). They highlight that despite the international acclaim gained by Aguas de Illamani for its successful design of a system suitable for the poor consumers, the levels of water consumption from this system are low because users in El Alto resist the installation of bathrooms, showers and laundries due to the extra costs involved, and prefer to utilise a single water point (normally in the central patio). These low levels of consumption, couples with the lack if slopes in El Alto, mean that the flow of water through the system is poor. As a result, the removal of sewerage is slow and blockages frequent, representing added health risks and producing unpleasant odours.

Health risks are further acerbated by the shallow tubing that is installed because it cannot withstand the weight of the trucks that pass by, leading to breakages and leakages, and compounding existing health problems. The low cost of the system is part premised on the use of community labour (Geoforum 2005). The repercussions of this are that community members are exposed to unhealthy conditions when undertaking repairs and general maintenance. If a community member does not fulfil their agreed maintenance responsibilities the whole system risk being vulnerable to general blockages with widespread negative impacts that provoke conflicts amongst neighbours. In some cases branches of the system are broken deliberately, the explanation being that residents do not want pipe work running through, or along the boundaries of their lots because this can affect future building plans.

These problems, i.e. the conflicts over ownership and management and the history of dams, place in question the advantages of large-scale, or externally imposed, projects, whether sewage systems or systems for water harvesting. Indeed, these questions are even more emphasised when one recognises that in many contexts effective small-scale and locally generated methods and techniques for water conservation and distribution are already available. Indeed, important experiments for local participation in the management of water supplies, that are not governed by outside interests and priorities, are currently taking place in Latin America[3].

In Brazil one of the most well-known example of participatory water management is the Departamento Municipal do Agua e Esgoto (DMAE), the water company of Porto Alegre which is the capital of the Rio Grande do Sul province in Southern Brazil. Water has been under public control in Porto Alegre since the Workers Party gained power in the city 15 years ago (Partido dos Trabalhadores, PT). DMAE is publicly

---

3. http://www.tni.org/

owned, but financially independent from the state and fully self-financed through the water bills paid by the 1.4 million inhabitants. It is a not-for-profit company that re-invests profits into improving the water supply. As in many other areas of public life in Porto Alegre and other parts of the Rio Grande do Sul, community members directly decide the budget priorities of their water company. Through a process of public meetings, every citizen can have a say in which new investments should be made first.[2] This participatory model is one of the reasons that poor communities in Porto Alegre have gained access to clean water: their needs are prioritised because they participate directly in deciding about new projects. Some 99.5% of the residents of Porto Alegre now have access to clean water, far more than anywhere else in Brazil.

A comparable participatory model is also in place in Rio Grande do Sul, where Companhia Riograndese do Saneamento (CORSAN) supplies around 6.5 million people. After the Worker's Party won the state elections in 1998, CORSAN was re-organised to give participatory budget assemblies a strong role in the company. Partly due to the involvement of around 80 'committees of users citizens', CORSAN is now considered one of the top-five most effective water companies in Brazil with an excellent record in expanding access to water.

In the late 1990s, Colombia's capital underwent a political revolution, with voters electing new independent and progressive governments. Against World Bank advice, the mayors of Bogotá, Enrique Peñalosa (1998–2000) and Antanas Mockus (2001–2003), decided the public's interest would be better served by strengthening the city's water and sewerage company, the EAAB, rather than by privatizing it. The Bogotá utility stands as an example of a crippled utility that turned itself around. In 1993, 78 percent of the people of Bogotá had clean drinking water and 70.8 percent had sewers. By the end of 2001, 95.2 percent had water services and 86.7 percent had sewers. In just eight years, despite massive migration, war and other violence, Bogotá reduced by 75 percent the number of households without running water and those without sanitation by more than half, according to the utility's 2001 annual report.

These new initiatives provide valuable alternative models for water management in the region. However, whilst applauding these new efforts, in this book we also argue that recuperation must also be made of the old. Whilst a large number of foreign and state initiated water management systems have failed for various reasons (Laurie 2005), locally developed water harvesting systems have proven their viability by surviving for hundreds of years. Whilst there has to be some recognition of the geographical limits and some questions asked about the quality of these water supplies, even with these detractors accounted for these systems often remain superior to those imposed by political and private interests, not only in terms of their reliability, but also in terms of their flexibility and more equitable control.

Responding to this problematic background, the aim of this book is then to demonstrate that such systems continue to offer cost-effective and viable methods and technologies for water harvesting. We question whether these methods and technologies are both transferable both within and without local communities? We also question whether such methods and technologies can be revived and even improved through dialogue between communities and with researchers of the type contributing here?

Modernity and New Social Formation

When discussing traditional systems the contributors to this book aim to stress that there are close ties in local peoples' minds between this concept and ideas and aspirations of modernity. Indeed, in the context of the Andes we recognise that because of historical transformations and the long impact of globalisation on local society and economy there is no easy seperation between tradition and modernity, or related ideas of culture and progress, rural and urban. Indeed, we argue that it is possible to observe in the militant response made to changes in national and local water management regimes, the generation of new social movements that support this complexity through a platform of tradition as modernity, and modernity as tradition. These movements break with previous political traditions and ideas of social movements[4] in terms of their rejection of partisan affiliations and in their gathering and focusing of support and demands from diverse sectors of the population.

Different indigenous movements in both Bolivia and Ecuador to greater or lesser degree now express this political complexity. This said it is perhaps the Bolivian formation of the *Coordinadora* that best expresses this transformation of political formation and relationship to modernity. As Assies describes in the case of the Cochabamba Water War, the Coordinadora emerged at a specific juncture as a loosely organised movement that from 1999 deployed a variety of initiatives and managed to gain broad sympathy among the population (Assies 2003). Although based on neighbourhood associations and civic committees, the Cochabamba Coordinadora was expanded across traditional class lines and beyond city limits through strategic alliances with producers' organisations. In the heat of the mobilisation, the Coordinadora brought together rural farmers, industrial proletariats, disillusioned recent in-migrants, largely invisible members of a growing informal economy, environmentalists, retirees, left-leaning economists and technocrats, as well as sympathetic foreigners in provincial towns, peripheral shanty towns and the urban streets in an ultimately successful and spectacular demonstration of popular consensus (Albro 2005).

Although started as a single-issue movement and retaining a network like structure, the town meetings, referendums and promotion of debate were actions of direct democracy that not only inspired the protests that resulted in the removal of the *Aguas de Tunari* concession and a review of Bolivian Water Law, but have been used to reconsider other issues such as electricity rates and the recovery of privatised state enterprises. In the course of 2000 to 2005 the idea of the Coordinadora spread and made an impact on the formation of political demand making elsewhere in the country.

In other parts of the country, like El Alto (see Poupeau in this volume for a notable exception), similar network-like structures have been developed in order to mobilise specific, but shared demands. Although the Movement for Socialism (MAS) and the Central Bolivian Union (COB) had a central role in the protests of 2003 it was not until other sectors joined in a Coordinadora that demonstrations reached the sufficient critical mass needed to topple the government. The National Coordination for the Defence of Gas mobilized 30,000 people in the Departments of Cochabamba and 50,000 in La Paz to demonstrate against the planned pipeline.

---

4. i.e. old (class, material) and new (single issue, rights based) movements.

As well as representing a new and successful kind of political formation in Bolivia, the Coordinadora also expresses the discursive relationship that exists between Andean ideas of tradition and modernity. The protesters in what have now become known as the Bolivian Water and Gas Wars stress their claims to «usos y costumbres» i.e. to culture and the usufruct rights to natural resources, something with build strongly on both revitalisation of cultural values and an appropriation of human rights language and ideas. In the Water protests the claim was made that «Bolivia's «traditional» communitarian values are under attack by the corrosively individualising hand of the market» (Olivera February 6, 2000). For underdeveloped peripheral neighbourhoods an Andean identity had become an effective idiom of distinction in directing claims for community resources. Indeed, we see in the protests that the wiphala (the Incan flag) has anchored the call for national cultural and natural sovereignty (Stephenson 2003).

Members of the Coordinadora and the closely allied irrigation associations (regantes) continue to practice rituals that thank mother earth, and retain a strong body of knowledge of water conservation and climate change to underpin their water management strategies and political demands (Crespo 2003). Andean tradition then forms an important base, but it is important to stress that despite its key role in the rhetoric of opposition leaders its understanding at the local level is mixed together with differing and non-oppositional notions of modernity. These ideas of modernity are particularly expressed in people's connected ideas of the global, their desires for improved rights as citizens and hopes for prosperity.

We are for example told by Laurie & Marvin (1999) that long before the Water conflict of 2000 the Misicuni Damn Project had become a regional dream. The privatization of water had introduced ideas of private ownership while creating the space to dream regional imaginations and to negotiate different definitions of 'the modern'. Support for Misicuni from the region and the region's resistance towards state efforts to establish a water contract suggested that there were clashing views of 'the modern'. One view of the modern 'neo-liberal water-trading» has been supported by the state and the other view of the modern «the big dam» has been supported by the region. This break-down of contrasting views of 'the modern' is further nuanced in Nina Laurie's study in this volume of the role of competing gender discourses in governing and transforming water management strategies and development regimes. Even though large scale integrated technical solutions were no longer thought practical and outdated in the context of the market economies of the 1990s, Misicuni had become emblematic of a particular regional identity, a perceived pathway to 'modernization' and the focus of a fight for independence.

Laurie & Marvin (ibid) highlight that the privatization and the particular nexus between globalization and neo-liberalism in Bolivia facilitated a dual approach towards these two clashing 'modern' logics of water. The privatization of the Bolivian water industry implies that neo-liberalism does not merely 'impact' upon the local. Rather, it is possible to see in some cases that neo-liberalism provides the opportunity for certain regional identities to be created and maintained while demanding respect for ideas which go against the outright logic of a liberalized economy. Such a conceptualization of neo-liberalism helps the dichotomy of the 'traditional' and the 'modern' to be surpassed and the boundary between the two previous sides of the dichotomy to become an interesting space for negotiation about contested meanings of 'the modern'.

Laurie & Marvin (ibid) comment further that this in-between space is, however, fragile because it places the people of Cochabamba in an awkward position, they do not want to give up their Misicuni dream and yet neither do they want to be represented as the 'country hicks' rejecting the 'modern' Bolivia. Hence, such concerns about representation in the fight over privatization suggest that the regional politics of resistance have needed to be very subtle. Privatization could not have been challenged on market grounds because that would have suggested that the Cochabamba community was 'anti-modern'. It could only be contested by appealing to cultural factors, including collective ownership of local water resources, and to the potential threat that privatization constituted for the Misicuni dream.

These insights into the formation of the Cochabamba Water protests help to counteract interpretations of the Bolivian crisis as the simple response of opposites, of indigenous culture to global pressures. Despite the continued reproduction of images of indigenous peoples in the development literature as backward, poor and isolated from world events, recent events in Bolivia demonstrate a completely different picture in which indigenous peoples are shown to be innovative and engaged with international actors and their concepts in the production and rules of local and national society. Moreover, they demonstrate that the indigenous and the global are linked, and that cultural responses cannot simply be derived from existing stereotypes of the traditional, or the Andean. Indeed, they break with the rigid dualism of earlier studies of modernity that counterpose individual and community, state and society, female and male to create modernity's distance from tradition. Lastly they underlines an observation that the local is not only deeply embedded in both the national and international, but that this involvement is also not necessarily oppositional.

The Bolivian Water and Gas Wars were sparked by a rejection of global economic policies and a desire to rethink the limits of national sovereignty. However, although the protests rejected the model of free trade and creation of concessions espoused by the government, the protesters were in general not opposed to the modernisation or the expansion of the international markets (McNeish 2006). Instead they were primarily aimed at forcing the government to guarantee sustainable access to natural resources, and secondly and perhaps more distantly to renegotiate the terms of trade and the democratic basis of the Bolivian state (See Poupeau in this volume).

The Story of this Book

It is within this much larger background or reservoir, that the following chapters of this book should be seen to fit. The book collects together papers presented by an international group of scholars at the first workshop hosted by the «Water Management in the Andes» network, based at the previous Centre for Environmental and Resource Management (SMR), now part of the Institute of Biology, University of Bergen. The workshop was held in October 2004 and funded by the Norwegian Research Council (NFR).

The workshop aimed to create a multi-disciplinary discussion focusing on the water resources in the region and as such brought together academics from a range of disciplinary backgrounds and specializations from the humanities, and social and natural sciences i.e. anthropology, sociology, biology, archaeology, history, agronomy and law.

As well as different disciplines the workshop also brought together academics from Bolivia and Ecuador as well as Norway, England, Spain and the United States. Indeed, as will be clear from the following description of contents the workshop attempted to include comparative study between the Andes region and other parts of the world. Through its casting up of both similarities and differences this effort at comparative study has not only helped to underline the validity of some of the authors' observations, but also highlighted an important future avenue for study by the network. Plans are now being made for comparative research on the historical and political dimensions of water technologies in Latin America, Southern Europe and the Middle East.

Given the quality and unexpected complementarity of contributions, as well as the interest shown in the workshop by students and established academics, it was decided by the two editors and contributors alike that an attempt should be made to form a publication representing the sum and depth of analysis made at this event. It is then the aim of this book to collect and capture the insight and results of this workshop and through doing so make a critical contribution to current understandings of water management, local knowledge, appropriate technology and participation in development. As well as producing a textbook for students within the University of Bergen's own Masters in Water Studies, it is also our aim to produce a book that can be used as a useful start-point by a wider community of teachers and students interested in the interlocking fields of water management, local knowledge and political ecology.

As will be obvious from the outline of chapters given below and our fragmented focus on only Ecuador and Bolivia, we do not claim to have produced a comprehensive study of Water Management in the Andean region. However, whilst not comprehensive in its geographical focus, or in its collecting together of information on local water management strategies in the region, it is our hope that by adopting an eclectic approach to the study of water management in which history, social change, national and international politics, economics, culture and gender are bound together we have produced a publication that underlines more clearly than past studies the multi-dimensional character and complexities of water resource management. As an interesting comparative case, and at the very end of this book, an article on local water management in ancient Near East civilizations is included in this volume. The article also introduces several important concepts in the study of natural resource management, including water harvesting. However, since this book is the result of both international and interdisciplinary cooperation, the way the various authors deals with these concepts will be coloured by their differences in background and perspectives.

Ecuador

The Ecuador section indeed owes very much to an interdisciplinary work going on from year 2000 to 2003 at the Ecuela Superior Politecnica del Litoral (EPOL) in Guayaquil, Ecuador, a work lead by the archaeologist Jorge Marcos, involving, besides archaeology, the fields of anthropology, botany, hydrology and palaeobotany. Two others of his team are also represented in his book, namely the anthropologists Silvia Alvarez and Martin Bazurco. Getting to know the project in its very final stage and being introduced to the research area and its people in the years to follow, the article by the anthropologist Frode F. Jacobsen provides more of an outsiders perspective on various water related projects by NGOs and state organizations on the Peninsula Santa Elena.

In «Water management in the ancient Ecuador» Jorge Marcos argues that early societies in ancient Ecuador developed in tune with the mega diversity that characterized the Holocene in this area c7800 BC. After a long period of Paleo-Indian (*Upper Palaeolithic*) living (c. 11 000 – 8500 BC.) and with the end of the Holocene the coast of Ecuador saw the development of an Archaic or *Neolithic Pre-ceramic* (8500–4000 BC.), followed by the formal *Neolithic* characterised by ceramic manufacture and the modification of the environment into a productive landscape. Marcos highlights that the important elements in the modification of the ecosystem to secure more stable production were earth constructions destined to manage rainfall, especially flooding (raised fields) and the runoff (detention ponds, so-called Albarradas), in areas where: 1. The floodplain remains under water a good part of the year; and 2. Where rainfall is low and with uncertain seasons of intensive rains. Marcos also reveals that an important local method of harvesting drinking water was to develop a system through which it was possible to condense and collect the moisture produced by the mist in the cloud forests of the Santa Elena Peninsula and Southern Manabí. In doing so Marcos's chapter reveals the extent of local innovation and the depth of local history that lies behind what are despite the passage of time are continuing practices for the collection and management of water.

In «Use and traditional knowledge of pre-Hispanic hydraulic systems among non-indigenous populations in the Ecuadorian coast» Silvia G. Alvarez describes the cistern and raised field systems and argues that they reveal the close relationship between local native societies and their natural environment in the Ecuadorian coast. She argues, however, that this relation is not understood by the majority of the population that currently benefits from the work and experience accumulated in these technological hydraulic systems. She contends that social devaluation and loss of knowledge, manifested especially among non-indigenous populations, are the result of newer power relations set in place by the Spanish authorities during the Colonial period.

The loss of native communities' power to decide over their territories and resources had a decisive effect on controlling and reproducing these technologies. Although these systems are efficient and are suitable for different environmental conditions, they have not been adapted to the social criteria that guide resource and manual labour exploitation, as established in most of the region. Hence, only territories under indigenous political leadership maintain and reproduce the technological capital inherited from «the ancient ones». In the other regions this native patrimony has been substituted by European experience and by the interests established by the requirements of political control and administration consolidated in country estates and plantations. At the same time that the subjects who produced pre-Colonial systems were being devaluated their knowledge was also being ignored. Ultimately, this has translated into the current population's detachment and loss of knowledge of available water management techniques. She argues that this also explains the lack of scientific research on native logics and products, and the privilege granted to technical and developmentalist techniques that are less environmentally sustainable and alien to local culture.

In «The future of the albarradas: between local knowledge and «development» policies» Claudia Gonzalez Andricaín focuses on the *comuneros* (members of the local communities) of the Ecuadorian coast and their use and reproduction of ancestral technologies for water provision, i.e. the *Albarradas*. She describes how various national and international NGOs operating on the Santa Elena Peninsula have acted to undermine the very livelihood of the local population through their interference with the Albarrada systems and by influencing and altering the framework of the communal organizations that are of vital social, cultural and ecological importance to the commoners. In spite of the existence of a rich and diverse eco-cultural patrimony in this region of Ecuador, the indigenous knowledge of local communities is rejected in spite of its documented historical effectiveness. Such rejection has had the consequence of eroding the local strategies and technologies of the local communities. In a context of social inequality in which local people now have differing levels of access to modern technologies and assistance the quality of life is also shown to have severely affected, poverty to have grown and local autonomy threatened.

In his chapter «Two stories about development on the Peninsula Santa Elena, Ecuador», Frode F. Jacobsen focuses on two development narratives that relate communities in the semi-arid area of the Ecuadorian Santa Elena Peninsula. Both stories deal with the aftermath of the local establishment of the British company *The Ancon Oil Company of Ecuador Limited* on La Punta de Santa Elena, on the tip of the peninsula, in 1911. He argues that these narratives are means of presenting the past in a way that imbue the present with meaning and create certain expectations about the future, shaping an experience of individual continuity and the continuity of ones culture and society. In outlining these narratives Jacobsen highlights how in their telling individuals contrast, rather than identify, themselves with other local individuals, and attempt to form contrasting «expert stories». He also uses their telling as a point of entry into a discussion of the two main conflicting views on native, local knowledge and local water and natural resource management on the peninsula, and how they influence and govern the lives of local people.

Bolivia

In «Negotiating Masculinities in the Water Sector» Nina Laurie explores how gendered representations and language help to structure development discourses, and as such play a role in both the consolidation and critique of accepted understandings of development orthodoxy. Through a discussion of the social and political relationships observed during the water protest and the campaign against Aguas de Tunari in Cochabamba, she explains the rupture of previous simplistic divisions between rural and urban, tradition and modernity, local and international as an outcome of overlapping and competing historic and contemporary expressions of masculinity. These are expressions of masculinity she shows to be closely tied to different scales of water management strategies and technologies (both practical and bureaucratic). In the course of her paper Laurie outlines the paternity, contradictions and weaknesses of each of these «heroic» masculinities as sources for competing versions of «the modern». Whilst she demonstrates that an international discourse on gender has at times the power to emasculate competing local discourses, she also highlights the impossibility of its hegemony in face of embedded local discourses and the rise of an international accept for a user-focused social development agenda. In this context, she concludes, that development projects and modernizing discourses cannot be consolidated, and consequently regimes of natural resource management remain informed by, but not frozen in, colonial and neo-colonial power relations.

In «Managing scarcity of water: Notes about political mobilisations in poor neighbourhoods of El alto, Bolivia» Frank Poupeau characterizes the basis and bases of the 2004 protests against the consortium water company, Aguas de Illimani, in El Alto, Bolivia. In this chapter Poupeua describes the origins and weaknesses of the Federación de Juntas Vecinales (FEJUVE), the local organization responsible for orchestrating the protests, set in a vivid account of the character and history of a city of migrants. Poupeau argues that contrary to recent media characterization the protests and this movement were not the result of a popular and undifferentiated out-pouring of anger against price increases and the intervention of foreign private capital. He demonstrates that the protests must be linked to a longer history of insurrection in Bolivia, as well as to longer traditions in social organization i.e. unions, neighborhood committees, and semi-clandestine political movements. Whilst stressing this, he also argues, however, that these movements and traditions never entirely encapsulate the public interest. This is a public interest, we are told, that whilst concerned with transformations at a larger scale, in a marginal community is first and foremost concerned with the mundane necessities of local survival (in this case clean drinking water).

Whilst individual and minimal survival strategies are put in practice, it is this persisting need that has made local people and neighborhoods vulnerable to the neo-liberal proposals and ideas of government multi-national companies. As a result collective solutions are abandoned and techno-commercial approaches are adopted in which the financing of the international development community takes up the slack of the limits and shortages left by the private companies who see no profit in extending their «comprehensive coverage» to peripheral areas. All of this Poupeau argues in conclusion creates a system of «two speeds» of installation, in which the services of established and wealthier neighborhoods are expanded and improved free of charge, but the services of marginal neighborhoods must await the coverage of labor costs and time through the «participation» of the poor themselves.

In «When the Solution of Irrigation became a Problem» Pablo Regalsky questions the current support of international donor organizations and NGOS for irrigation schemes, a policy that has developed in reaction to the previously social and environmental disasters of earlier mega-dam projects. Despite the accepted current wisdom of small irrigation schemes, through an outline and discussion of the results of a integrated development project funded by the Inter-American Development Bank (BID), Regalsky highlights the serious social consequences that can occur as a result of the careless introduction of new micro irrigation technologies. Through reference to the differential introduction of this project in three communities in the Cochabamba Valley, he demonstrates what appear to be contradictory outcomes.

Where agriculture production is improved there is also an increase in out-migration. Indeed, in the communities where agricultural output is improved, he also draws out attention to a surprising rise in local suicide rates. Regalsky explains these apparent contradictions as the result of the longer terms impact of new technologies on social networks and household economies. He also argues that the change to new irrigation systems and kinds of seeds has made local farmers in these communities overly reliant on loans and other forms of outside assistance- assistence that is never consistent or sustained. Regalsky also indicates that the failure of these irrigation technologies and of outside assistance might well have fueled the discontent of local irrigation associations (*regantes*) and assisted their radicalisation, involvement and central role in the Bolivian Water War of 2000.

Small-scale water harvesting in the Ancient Near East: A comparative case

In «Local Level Water Management and the Progress of Civilizations in the Ancient Near East» Øystein LaBianca demonstrates that many of the cultural history and politicization of water management has been and continues to be central to the formation of civilizations and modern development of the Near East as the have and are in Latin America. LaBianca highlights through a review of literature and histories of Southern Mesopotamia, Egypt, and the Levant that similar tension between «large» and small» traditions for water management were equally visible in the Ancient East as they are in present-day Bolivia and Ecuador. LaBianca argues that the progress and development of various civilizations in the Ancient Near East depended as much on, and perhaps even more, on local control of water as they did state level controls. This, he claims, is because local level systems are far more resilient and thus less vulnerable to exhaustion and collapse. This provides growing civilizations with a more stable and consistent stratum on top of which successive dynasties and state projects can rise and fall.

LaBianca's main thesis then is that Great and Little Traditions cooperate to produce long-term cycles of intensification and abatement in local food systems which, in turn, are reflected in changes over time and space in historical landscapes and in region-wide and local policies and practices for controlling water resources. He claims that these observations provide lessons for modern water management. Since expert knowledge is normally required by states to build and maintain large-scale and widespread infrastructure, the presumption tends to take hold within state bureaucracies that expert knowledge is automatically to be preferred over local or indigenous knowledge. This presumption, and associated sentiments about the inferiority of local knowledge, can and does lead to policies and practice that undermine or actively seek to destroy local practice. However, this typical turn of events also ignores the important role that local traditional practice have in sustaining larger systems and therefore elites, through periods of economic difficulty and political turmoil. For development to be sustainable there is then need for a common acceptance of the co-existence of both large and small scale traditions.

Bibliography

Alarcón-Cháires (2003) *Plan-Puebla Panama: Crítica desde la perspectiva rural y ambiental a una política de estado de combate a la pobreza.* Unpublished paper.

Álvares, S.G. (2002). *Etnicidades en la Costa Ecuatoriana.* Quito, Ecuador: Abya Yala.

Anderson, R.B. (1997) «Corporate/indigenous partnerships in economic development: the First Nations in Canada». *World Development* 25(9):1483ff.

Ascher, W. y Hubbard, A. (1989) *Recuperación y Desarrollo en Centroamérica. Ensayos del Grupo Especial de la Comisión Internacional para la Recuperación y el Desarrollo en Centroamérica.* San José. Costa Rica. pp.111–120.

Barbier, E.B (2000) Links between liberalisation and rural resource degradation in the developing regions. *Agricultural Economics* 23 (3):299–310.

Babiker, M. (1996). Management of aridity: Water conservation and procurement in Dar Hamar, Western Sudan. In A.G.M. Ahmad and H.A. Abdel Ati (eds.): *Managing scarcity. Human adaptation in East African drylands.* OSSREA.

Barlow, M. & Clarke, T. 2002. *Blue gold: The battle against corporate theft of the world's water.* London: Earthscan.

Bicker, A. (2004). *Development and local knowledge: new approaches to issues in natural resources management, conservation and agriculture.* London: Routledge.

Buitelaar RM, Perez RP (2000) Maquila, economic reform and corporate strategies. World Development 28 (9): 1627–1642 SEP.

Blackburn, J. 2000. *Popular participation in a prebendal society: A case study of participatory municipal planning in Sucre, Bolivia.* Doctoral thesis. Sussex: University of Sussex.

Blackburn, J, Chambers, C & Gaventa, J. (2000) Mainstreaming Participation and Development, in OED Working Papers Series 10. Washington DC. World Bank.

Bloch, M. 1986. *From Blessing to Violence: History and ideology in the circumcision ritual of the Merina of Madagascar.* Cambridge: Cambridge University Press.

Brook Cowen, P. and N. Tynan. (1999). «Reaching the Urban Poor with Private Infrastructure.» in *Public Policy for the Private Sector*, No 188.

Blunt, P. and D.M Warren (1996) (Eds.) *Indigenous Organizations and Development.* London: Intermediate Technology Publications.

Burgete Cal y Mayor, A. 2000. *Indigenous Autonomy in Mexico.* Copenhagen: International Work Group for Indigenous Affairs.

Burns, Hambleton & Hoggart (eds) (1994) The Politics of Decentralisation: Revitalising Local Democracy. Macmillan: London.

Bøe, J. (2002). «*Jordbruket vil alltid forbli den beste jobben, det var det som var den første kjærligheten*»: *en komparativ sosialantropologisk studie av irrigasjonssamfunn på Vestbredden.* Master thesis in social anthropology. Bergen: University of Bergen.

Calva, L., 1996. La reforma económica de México y sus impactos en el sector agropecuario. En: p. Bovin (ed.), El campo mexicano: una modernización a marchas forzadas, México, D.F.:31–75.

Campbell, B. (2005). Changing protection policies and ethnographies of environmental engagement. *Conservation and Society 2,* Vol.3, pp.280–322.

Cavalcanti, C (2002) Economic Thinking, Traditional Ecological Knowledge and Ethnoeconomics. Current Sociology January Vol 50(1): 39–55. Sage Publications: London.

Chambers, R (1997) Whose Reality Counts? Putting the First Last. Intermediate Technology: London.

Chambers, R. (1994). The origins and practice of participatory rural appraisal. *World Development* 22(7), 953–969.

Coleman, J.S. (1988) Social Capital in the Creation of Human-Capital. *American Journal of Sociology* 94: S95-S120 Suppl. S.

Comisión Económica para América Latina y el Caribe (CEPAL), 1994. Tipología de productores agrícolas de los ejidos y comunidades en México. México, 172 pp.

Cooke, B & Kothari, U (2001) *Participation: The New Tyranny?* Zed Book: London & New York.

Cornell, S. and J.P Kalt (eds.) (1992) *What Can Tribes Do? Strategies and Institutions in American Indian Economic Development*. Los Angeles: American Indian Studies Center, UCLA.

Crespo, C (2003) 'Continuidad y Ruptura: La Guerra del Agua y los nuevos Movimientos Sociales en Bolivia', Revista del Observatorio Social de America Latina. 2. CLACSO: Buenos Aires.

Cruz, M.C. and Medina, R.S. (2003). *Agriculture in the city: a key to sustainability in Havana, Cuba*. Ian Randle Publishers.

Cunningham, K (2003) Frihandelens skjeve fordeling- en lekse fra Mexico, *LAG Newsletter* Nr3 October.

Crook R. C & Manor, J (1998) *Democracy and Decentralisation in South Asia & West Africa: Participation, Accountability and Performance*. CUP: Cambridge.

D'Andrade, R. (1995). *The development of cognitive anthropology*. Cambridge, Mass.: Cambridge University Press.

Dollar, D (2001) Globalisation, inequality and poverty since 1980. World Bank 2001.

Dougherty, J. and Keller, C. (1982). Taskonomy: a practical approach to knowledge structures. *American Ethnologist 4*, Vol.9, pp.763–774.

Ellen, R. et al. (2000) *Indigenous knowledge and its transformations: critical anthropological perspectives*. Amsterdam: Harwood Academic Publ.

Ellen, R. (1993). *The cultural relations of classification. An analysis of Nuaulu animal categories from central Seram*. Cambridge, Mass.: Cambridge University Press.

Eversole, R, Ridgeway, L & Mercer, D. (2005) Indigenous Anti-Poverty Strategies in an Australian Town. In Eversole, McNeish & Cimadamore (eds) *Indigenous Peoples and Poverty*: An International Perspective. CROP Series. Zed Books: London

Egziabher, A. et al., eds. (1994). *Cities feeding people: an examination of urban agriculture in East Africa*. Ottawa, Canada: IDRC.

Fairchild, J & Leach, M (1998) Reframing deforestation: global analyses and local realities with studies in West Africa. Routledge: New York.

Fals Borda, O (1998) People's Participation: challenges ahead. New York: Apex Press.

Fine, B (1999) The Development State is Dead- Long live Social Capital? Development andChange 30 (1): 1–19

Gerbrandy, G. and Hoogendam, P. (1998). *Aguas y acequias. Los derechos al agua y la gestion campesina de riego en los Andes bolivianos*. La Paz, Bolivia: Plural Editors.

Goffman, E. 1962. *Asylums. Essays on the Social Situation of Mental Patients and Other Inmates.* Chicago: Aldine Publishing Company.

Goldin, L.R. (1996) «Economic Mobility strategies among Guatemalan peasants: prospects and limits of nontraditional vegetable cash crops», Human Organization 55(1):99–100.

Harris, J & de Renzio, P (1997) Policy Arena: Missing Link or Analytically Missing? The Concept of Social Capital. Journal of International Development 9 (7): 919–37.

Healy, K. (2001) Llamas, Weavings, and Organic Chocolate: Multicultural Grassroots Development in the Andes and Amazon of Bolivia. Notre Dame, Indiana: University of Notre Dame Press.

Heath, J., 1988. El financiamiento del sector agropecuario en México. En: Colegio de Michoacán y CONACYT (eds.), Las Sociedades Rurales Hoy, México:129–142.

Hickey, S. and Mohan, G. (eds) (2004) Participation: From Tyranny to Transformation? Zed Books: London & New York.

Hirschman, Albert O. (1984). Getting Ahead Collectively: Grassroots Experiences in Latin America, Elmsford, NY: Pergamon Press.

Ife, J. (2002) *Community development: Community-based alternatives in an age of globalisation* (second edition). Frenchs Forest, NSW: Pearson Education Australia.

IUCN/WCPA/WWF (The World Conservation Union/World Commission on Protected Areas/World Wildlife Fund for Nature) (2000) 'Indigenous and Traditional Peoples and Protected Areas: Principles, Guidelines and Cases Studies'. Best Protected Area Guidelines Series No. 4.

Jacobsen, Frode F. 1998. *Exploring theories of sickness and misfortune among the Hadandowa Beja. Narratives as points of entry into Beja cultural knowledge.* London: Kegan Paul International.

James, Wendy. (1999). Empowering ambiguities. I: Angela Cheater (red.): *The anthropology of power: empowerment and disempowerment in changing structures.* London: Routledge, s.13–27.

Keare, D.H. (2001) «Learning to Clap: Reflections on Top-Down versus Bottom-Up Development», Human Organization 60(2):159–165.

Keesing, Roger M. 1975. *Cultural Anthropology.* New York: Holt, Rinehart and Winston.

Korovkin, T. (1998) «Commodity Production and Ethnic Culture: Otavalo, Northern Ecuador. *Economic Development and Cultural Change* 47(1):125–154.

Laurell A.C & Wences. M. I (1994) Do Poverty Porgrams Alleviate Poverty- The Case of the Mexican National Solidarity Program. International Journal of Health Services 24 (3): 381–401.

Laurie, Nina. 2005. Establishing development orthodoxy: negotiating masculinities in the water sector. *Development and Change*, 36(3), 527–549

Laurie, N. and Marvin, S. 1999. Globalisation, neo-liberalism and negotiated development in the Andes: Bolivian water and the Misicuni dream. 31. *Environment and Planning*, 31, 1401–1415

Laurie, N. et al. (2002). The excluded 'indigenous'? The implications of multi-ethnic politics for water reform in Bolivia. In Rachel Sieder (ed.): *Multiculturalism in Latin America. Indigenous rights, diversity and democracy.* Baringstoke: Palgrave Macmillan, pp.252–276.

Lee Van Cott, D (2000) The Friendly Liquadatio of the Past: The Politics of Diversity in Latin America. University of Pittsburgh Press. Pittsburgh.

Marcos, J. et al. (2004). *Agua y Biodiversidad. Manejo y Uso Sostenible. Albarradas y Biodiversidad en la Costa.* Guayaquil, Ecuador: ESPOL and Banco Mundial publication.

Marshall, L. (1976) Sharing, talking, and giving: relief of social tenstions, chapter 9 in *The!Kung of Nyae Nyae*, Cambridge, Mass.: Harvard Univ. Press.

Martinez, J.A (1996) Municipios y Participación Popular en America Latina: Un modello de Dessarrollo. IAF/SEMILLA/CEBIAE: La Paz.

Marvin S. and Laurie, N. An Emerging Logic of Urban Water Management in Cochabamba, Bolivia. *Urban Studies* 1999, 36(2), 341–357.

McCaskill, D. 1997, From Tribal Peoples to Ethnic Minorities: The Transformation of Indigenous Peoples» in McCaskill and Kampe (eds) Development or Domestication? Indigenous Peoples of Southeast Asia. Chiang Mai: Silkworm Books.

McBride, J. (Ed.) (2001) «Our Own Vision – Our Own Plan, What Six First Nations Organisations have accomplished with their own Economic Development Plans.» Burnaby, British Colombia: Community Economic Development Centre, Simon Fraser University, available on the Internet at http://www.sfu.ca/cedc/abced/Our_Own_Vision8.pdf.

McNeish, J (2006) Stones on the Road: The Politics of Participation and the Generation of Crisis in Bolivia. Bulletin of Latin American Research. Vol 25:1.

McNeish, J (2002) Globalisation and the Reinvention of Andean Tradition: The Politics of Community and Ethnicity in Highland Bolivia. The Journal of Peasant Studies Volume 29, No 3/4 April/July. Frank Cass: London & New York.

McNeish, J (2001) Pueblo Chico, Infierno Grande: Globalization and the Politics of Participation in Highland Bolivia. Unpublished PhD. University of London.

Molyneux M (2002) Gender and the Silences of Social Capital: Lessons from Latin America. Development and Change 33 (2): 167–188.

Mohan, G (1996) Neoliberalism and decentralised development planning in Ghana. Third World Planning Review 18, No.4. 433–454.

Mohan, G. and Stokke, K. (2000). Participatory development and empowerment: the dangers of localism. *Third World Quarterly*, 21 (2), 247–268.

Mougeot, L.J.A. (1994). *Urban food production: evolution, official support and significance.* Ottawa, Canada: IDRC.

Nelson, N & Wright, S. (1995) Power and Participatory Development: Theory and Practice. Intermediate Technology: London.

Nickson, Andrew (2001b) «Tapping the market-can private enterprise supply water to the poor?» *ID21 Insights*, Issue No 37.

Overseas Development Institute (2003) Identifying better rural development strategies in Honduras and Nicaragua. ODI Report.

OXFAM (2003) Dumping without Borders: How US agricultural policies are destroying the livelihoods of Mexican corn farmers. Oxfam: UK.

Parry, J. (1986). The Gift, the Indian Gift and the «Indian gift». *Man*, vol. 21.no.3

Parry, J. & Bloch, M., 1989. Introduction: Money and the morality of exchange. In Jonathan Parry & Maurice Bloch (eds.): *Money and the Morality of Exchange.* Cambridge: Cambridge University Press, pp 1–32.

Partridge, W.L. and Jorge E. Urquillas, with Kathryn Johns. (1996) «Including the Excluded: Ethnodevelopment in Latin America» paper presented at the Annual World Bank Conference on Development in Latin America and the Caribbean, Bogotá, Colombia.

Polanyi, K. 1944. *The great transformation.* New York: Farrar & Rinehart.

Portes, A (1998) Social Capital: its origins and application in modern society. Annual Review of Sociology 24: 1–24.

Posey, D.A (2002) Kayapó ethnoecology and culture. In Plenderleith (ed) Studies in environmental anthropology vol. 6Routledge: London.

Posey, D.A (2000) Exploitation of bio-diversity and indigenous knowledge in Latin America: challenges to sovereignty and the old order, In Cavalcanti (ed) The Environment, Sustainability and Public Policies:Building Sustainability in Brazil. Cheltenham: Edward Elgar, pp-186–209.

Pradhan, P. and Gautam, U. (2002). *Farmer managed irrigation systems in the changed context: proceedings of the second international seminar held on 18–19 April 2002, Katmandu, Nepal.* Katmandu: Farmer Managed Irrigation Systems Promotion Trust.

Putnam, R (1993) Making Democracy Work: Civic Traditions in Modern Italy. Pronceton University Press.

Ramos, A.R. (1998) *Indigenism: Ethnic Politics in Brazil.* Madison: University of Wisconsin Press.

Robins-Lino, T. (2000) Los Mayangnas y la Reserva de la Biosfera de Bosawas. Memoria de la Segunda Jornada Indígena Centroamericana sobre Tierra, Medio Ambiente y Cultura, San Jose, C. R.:461–463.

Sánchez- Pérez, H. Morales Guadalupe. V, Escudero Alberto & N, María Jansá. J. (2003) Condiciones de Vida y Salud de la Mujer en Zonas de Alta marginación socioeconómica de Chiapas, Mexico: ¿ Es Peor ser indígena?. Forthcoming: *Indigenous Peoples and Poverty: Identity, Autonomy and Inclusion.* CROP Series. Zed Books.

Sánchez, R. (2000) Manejo de áreas protegidas en Belice: el movimiento hacia el comanejo comunal. Memoria de la Segunda Jornada Indígena Centroamericana sobre tierra, Medio Ambiente y Cultura, San Jose, C. R.:464–467.

Seabrook, J (2003) The No-nonsense Guide to World Poverty. New Internationalist: Oxford.

Sieder, R. and Witchell, J. (2001). Advancing indigenous claims through the law: reflections on the Guatemalan peace process. In Jane Cowan *et al.* (eds.): *Culture and rights: anthropological perspectives.* Cambridge University Press, pp.201–225.

Sikkink, L (1997) El Poder Mediador Del Cambio de Aguas: Género y El Cuerpo Político Condeño. In Arnold, D (ed) *Más allá del Silencio: Las Fronteras de Género en Los Andes* CIASE/ILCA: La Paz

Simonelli, J. and D. Earle (2003) «Disencumbering Development: Alleviating Poverty Through Autonomy in Chiapas,» in *Here to Help, NGOs Combating Poverty in Latin America*, ed. R. Eversole, Armonk, New York: M.E. Sharpe.

Smit, J. et al. (1996). *Urban agriculture, food, jobs, and sustainable cities.* New York: UNDP.

Smith, Warrick (2000) «Regulating Infrastructure for the Poor. Perspectives on Regulatory System Design.» in *Infrastructure for Development: Private Solutions and the Poor Conference*. London: World Bank, 17 pp.

Smith, C. (1984) «Does a Commodity Economy Enrich the Few While Ruining the Masses? Differentiation Among Petty Commodity Producers in Guatemala.» *Journal of Peasant Studies* 11(3):60–95.

Spiro, Melford E. 1986. Some reflections on cultural determinism and relativism with special reference to emotion and reason. In Richard A. Shweder and Robert A. LeVine: *Culture Theory. Essays on Mind, Self and Emotion*. Cambridge: Cambridge University Press, pp. 323–346.

Strathern, Marilyn. 1980. No nature, no culture. In Carol MacCormack & Marilyn Strathern (eds.): *Nature, Culture and Gender*. UK: Cambridge University Press.

Strauss, Claudia. 1997. Research on cultural discontinuities. In Claudia Strauss & Naomi Quinn (eds.): *A cognitive theory of cultural meaning*. N.Y.: Cambridge University Press.

Tendler, J., 1999 *Good Government in the Tropics*. Baltimore: Johns Hopkins University Press.

Toledo, V. M., 2000. La Paz en Chiapas: luchas indígenas de inspiración ecológica. Edit. Quinto Sol., México. 256 pp.

Toledo, V., 1988. La sociedad rural, los campesinos y la cuestión ecológica. En: Colegio de Michoacán y CONACYT (eds.), Las Sociedades Rurales Hoy, México: 273–285.

Tynan, N. (2000). «Private Participation in Infrastructure and the Poor: Water and Sanitation.», in *Infrastructure for Development: Private Solutions for the Poor Conference*. London.

Usher, A. D. (ed.). 1997. *Dams as aid: A political economy of the Nordic development thinking*. London: Routledge.

Varisco, D. M. (1982). *The adaptive dynamics of water allocation in Al.-Ahjur, Yemen Arab Republic*. PhD dissertation. Ann Arbor, Mich.: University of Pennsylvania.

Water and Sanitation Program -South Asia (2001) *The Buenos Aries Concession. The Private Sector Serving the Poor,* New Delhi: Water and Sanitation Program. South Asia.

Webster N (2002) In the Name of the Poor: contesting political space for poverty reduction. New York: Zed Books.

Weiner, A. B. (1988) *The Trobrianders of Papua New Guinea*, New York: Holt, Rinehart & Winston

Wiessner, P. (1981) «Risk, reciprocity and social influences on!Kung San economics» in Eleanor Leacock and Richard Lee (eds.), *Politics and History in Band Societies*, Cambridge: Cambridge University Press.

Wilson, P. (2003) «Market Articulation and Poverty Eradication? Critical Reflection on Tourist-Oriented Craft Production in Amazonian Ecuador» in *Here to Help, NGOs Combating Poverty in Latin America*, ed. R. Eversole, Armonk, New York: M.E. Sharpe.

Woolcock, M (1998) Social capital and economic development: Toward a theoretical synthesis and policy framework. Theory and Society 27 (2): 151–208.

Part I

Introduction Part I: Albarradas in Coastal Ecuador: Rescuing Traditional Knowledge on Sustainable Use of Biodiversity[5]

Jorge G. Marcos

The advances of warm water produce seasonal rains in south west Ecuador and in northern Peru, this phenomenon is known as the «El Niño Southern Oscillation» (ENSO). The climate of this area is characterized by the northern-most influence of the Humboldt Current, which is expected to give way to advances of the warm waters from the Panamanian current from December to May. The rivers in the area are dry most of the year. When it rains, during a normal rainy season, they can flood for a short time, and then they run a trickle of water until the next rain. Rains can be totally absent for several years, but when hard seasonal rains, or an El Niño event occur, most of the water from the run-off is lost into the sea. During these events some of the aquifers are recharged in some areas like at the Point of Santa Elena, but in most of the area more water runs off into the sea than sinks into the aquifer.

In the pre-Columbian past, the people of the Santa Elena Peninsula developed adaptive strategies in the face ENSO events. To capture water from the run-off, they built what is now known in the area as «Albarradas», «jagueyes» or «tareas» (tasks). These are horseshoe shaped earth embankments with the borrow pit in its center and its opening facing the incline to trap rainwater from the run-off. The purpose of building the Albarradas was to trap water from the run-off and allow it to sink into the aquifer, which was used through several methods. The water stored in the aquifer by the Albarradas was tapped through wells excavated to one side of the Albarrada embank-

---
5. Medium Size GEF Project

ment and sometime at the center of vase. In large systems, like Muey, sunken fields were excavated close to the water table in order to plant on the humidified surface.

Rescuing knowledge of indigenous people is key in improving our understanding of sustainability issues in biodiversity. As explained above, Pre-Columbian societies developed sophisticated systems to respond to ecological fluctuations and, in some places, were able to conserve biodiversity and fine-tune benign interaction with their environment. In the context of an area of ecological importance, but in a situation of fragility, the objective of this project is directed to the recuperation, conservation and protection of the Albarrada system. Socio-environmental research undertaken by the project will allow to measure changes in local biodiversity through time, as well as increase our understanding of pre-Columbian techniques used to manage biodiversity, including wild relatives of cultivars. This work allowed social and natural scientists (ethno-botanists, agronomists, socio-cultural anthropologists, hydrologists, civil engineers, geologists and archeologists) to delineate strategies to rescue these techniques and apply them in a modern context, and to provide basic information and actions to conserve these wild relatives. The recovery of this water harvesting and management technology should also turn into an economic asset for the native communities in the area, for the use of Albarradas not only does conserve water, but raises the freactic level close to surface. This favors the sustainability of the natural plant cover and traditional agriculture, which at present has relapsed due to the lack of maintenance of the Albarrada system. The Albarradas project decidedly contributes to the rational and sustainable management of the region (see Álvarez (this volume), Marcos (this volume), and Gonzalez (this volume)).

Trans-disciplinary research by social and natural scientist has clarified in what way newly constructed Albarradas differ form the traditional ones, in terms of placement in the landscape, in relation to fluvial and surface runoff, in their design and in their core construction, among others. This has permitted to increase our understanding of the Albarradas system as sustainable use responses to this environment today. This line of enquiry also addressed how have traditional common property resource management systems have changed in response to the changing social, economic and political context and how has this affected the knowledge base and practices relating to the construction, maintenance, management of natural vegetation and agriculture.

Ecuadorian dry tropical forests are made up of a series of different micro environments which are endangered by several forms of human activities (i.e. road construction, deforestation). In each one of these micro environments ancient albarradas occur, and most albarradas are relicts to native plants and cultigens. Plant collection in each one of these albarradas and environs has secured seeds and cuttings of existent vegetal cover biodiversity. Archaeological and ethno-botanical procedure focussing on the reconstruction of the history of plant cover variation in the area and the use of native cultivars, was basic to this project, and is basic to any successful sustainable development program and sustainable management of biodiversity in the area. Some communities still make use of albarradas and there are living members who recall their more recent past use. Thus anthropological research was also important to complete the picture, as well as to prepare the dissemination of results among the native communities in the study area.

This knowledge is a critical input to enhance our understanding of factors affecting biodiversity sustainability and therefore has made a substantial contribution to improving GEF's methods and approaches described in its Operational Programs (See Annex 2). It is expected that this interdisciplinary form of research on traditional knowledge and technologies may be replicated in other areas around the world where similar problems of water-resource management and biodiversity conservation are found.

Geographic Characterization of the Area

The Project study-area is geographically located in the southwestern coastal plain of Ecuador. It is placed on the littoral of southern Manabí and Guayas provinces. It spreads from the coastal cordilleras western divide to the Pacific Ocean, covering approximately an area of 4,500 Km2. The project area covers an important portion of the dry forests of the Pacific Coast of South America. Ecuadorian dry tropical forests are known for its high levels of both regional and local endemism. This ecoregion is considered critical, globally outstanding and of highest priority at the Regional Scale.

Because it presents a wide variety of dry tropical forests, the coastal region is considered as a biotic province and a priority area for dry tropical forest research. It possesses an extremely diverse flora, and is a place with an extreme composition of endemic (20%) plants, containing species with restricted distribution and/or endangered species, both at national and world levels. A distinctive peculiarity is the variety of micro-habitats it possesses with a great variety of physical characteristics, a probable cause for its naturally endemic richness. In this area the Machalilla National Park, protected under the Protected Zone Regime, is found.

The specific ecoregion where the project takes place has been classified as an Ecoregion of Highest Priority and is classified as the northern section of the Tumbes/Piura dry forest, this is part of the Tropical Broadleaf Forest, which encompasses the Ecuadorian dry forests (Ecuador) and the Tumbes/Piura dry forest (Ecuador, Peru) (Valverde, 1979, 1991, 1998). This region is influenced by complex seasonal changes, due to variations in marine currents, atmospheric circulation, and thermal inversion that interact with a mountainous chain that runs parallel to the Pacific. Other factors are man-made, like severe deforestation, due to charcoal-making practices, oil exploration and exploitation and more recently by shrimp farming operations. It is considered an ecologically fragile area; the unique dry tropical forest of the Ecuadorian coast needs urgently a program for the conservation and sustainable management of its biodiversity.

The *Chongón – Colonche* Cordillera, with elevations of more than 800 m. is covered by coastal fogs or «*garúas*» from May to October due to thermal inversion caused by the lowering of sea water temperatures, produce changes in climate and vegetation. A combination natural and social factor have promoted the destruction of these ecosystems, and a displacement of native crops for introduced species due to the «modernization» of traditional agricultural practices, resulting in the accelerated disappearance of genetic resources stored in the native species and varieties. Although, under certain conditions, the promotion of unconventional species and varieties developed under biotechnological processes may increment production, the uniformity of such plants can result in a massive loss of crops due to pests, plagues, draughts, or floods. In this sense the *Albarradas* and their environs are a refuge to genetic varieties now absent elsewhere in the area.

According to the modern definition of Wetlands *[Humedales] Albarradas* are considered artificial wetlands that have contributed to the sustainable use of natural resources, converted into important means for water management directed to herding and agriculture in the dry areas of southwestern Ecuador.

It is expected that the soil samples obtained from limited excavations in *Albarradas* will render fossil evidence of the vegetal cover surrounding the site and that our proposed research will permit comparisons between the paleo-botanical cover and the vegetation found there today. It is expected that we find relics of wild relatives of cultivated plants surviving around ancient *Albarradas*, or certify their disappearance in the area. Conservation of genetic resources of cultivated plants is indispensable to plant improvement, and these are not always found in protected areas, since they have evolved to survive droughts, or floods.

Genetic identification and conservation are the most important objectives to plan for a future reforestation program that may truly reproduce the dry tropical forest diversity, characteristic of the area. These results would be extremely useful for national reforestation programs currently being designed by the Ministry if Environment and local projects like the ESPOL development plan for the Santa Elena Peninsula.

Description of the albarradas system

Geologically, the area from the Santa Elena Peninsula (Ecuador) to Talara (Peru) is distinguished by its Tablazo formation, characterized by Pleistocene marine terraces that have up-lifted in three different stages since the lower Pleistocene. The Tablazo formation rests on a Tertiary substrate and constitutes the uppermost aquifer, where rain water is naturally stored.

Apparently the earliest *Albarradas* were built in San Pablo, associated with a Late Valdivia occupation (map. 2) (c. 2000–1800 BC) (Marcos 1988). The most spectacular set of *Albarradas* are found between the village of Muey and the Port of La Libertad (McDougle 1967), one of these, the Albarrada of Achallán has been dated by Stothert (1995) to the Engoroy period (c. 850–300 BC) (Bushnell, 1951).

There were about 250 *Albarradas* in Muey and were mapped by MacDougle in 1967. They are also quite evident in aerial photographs taken in the sixties and seventies. In the center of the Village of Muey -as well as in the northeast sector of La Libertad- a series of continuous excavations into the top of the aquifer created and artificial «river». Its manmade beaches served to plant cultivars that require much humidity, creating a tropical garden in an otherwise arid area.

Representatives from the 12 Communes that attended the 1st Workshop on Albarradas mentioned that some *Albarradas* were destroyed by the ENSO event of 1982–83. Others, they said, went down during the 1997–98 *Mega-Niño*, while those that resisted and kept functioning were *Albarradas* which they referred as «*de la antiguedad*» (probably pre-Columbian). While those they referred to as «*de la nueva era*» (built or refurbished recently by official institutions like Inheri or Municipalities) had been severely damaged or completely destroyed. It is important to test this hypothesis and compare the ancient and modern modes of building *Albarradas* and their placement in the landscape.

Preliminary observations show that modern *Albarradas* that have been built with the assistance of technical personnel from official institutions, using heavy equipment, and were generally placed trying to maximize water-catchments, by blocking higher order rivers. Older *Albarradas* built by the native communities in the past were placed in the lower order, barely catching the superficial runoff before the arroyos or on *pampas* before rainwater reaches the seashore. The modern *Albarradas* have been apparently destroyed by the added pressure placed on their embankment by the excessive amount of water collected during strong ENSOs. The excess water sometimes cut-into the drainage channels eroding them to a level that rendered the *Albarradas* useless, or completely destroyed the embankment. It is necessary to research, with the aid of aerial photography and satellite images, the logic behind the placement of ancient *Albarradas*, in order to confirm what geographical/geological aspects and features were considered in the past to define their successful position with relation to the landscape.

References

Álvarez, Silvia

1998 Recuperación y defensa de territorio étnico en la Costa ecuatoriana: el caso de la Antigua Comunidad de Indígenas de Chanduy, en: Hombre y Ambiente, el Punto de Vista Indígena (8): Abya-Yala, Quito.

1989 *Tecnología Prehispánica, Naturaleza y Organización Cooperativa en la Cuenca del Guayas.* Colección Peñón del Río 4, Ed. Centro de Estudios Arqueológicos y Antropológicos, ESPOL, Guayaquil, Ecuador.

1990 Campos de Camellones: la naturaleza modificada a través de la historia, en: *Revista Geográfica,* Instituto Geográfico Militar 28: 153–163 Quito

1991 Los Comuneros de Santa Elena. Tierra, Familia y Propiedad. Biblioteca de Ciencias Sociales Vol. 34, Corporación Editorial Nacional, Abya-Yala, Quito.

Bushnell, Geoffrey H. S. 1951. *The Archaeology of the Santa Elena Peninsula in South West Ecuador. Cambridge, Cambridge University Press.*

Marcos, Jorge G. 1988. Real Alto: La Historia de un Centro Ceremonial Valdivia *Biblioteca Ecuatoriana de Arqueología.* Vols. 4 y 5. ESPOL/Corporación Editora Nacional, Quito.

McDougle, Eugene 1967 Water use and Settlements in Changing Environments of the Southern Ecuadorian Coast. Submitted in Partial Fulfillment of the Requirements for the Degree of Master of Art, in the Faculty of Political Science, Columbia University

Stothert, Karen 1995. Las Albarradas tradicionales y el manejo de aguas en la Península de Santa Elena, en: Miscelánea Antropológica ecuatoriana, Boletín del Área Cultural del Banco Central del Ecuador, 8:131–160, Guayaquil, Ecuador.

Valverde, Flor de María; GR. Tazán y C. García 1979. Cubierta Vegetal en la Península de Santa Elena. Facultad de Ciencias Naturales. Universidad de Guayaquil.

Valverde, Flor de María; G. Rodríguez y C. García 1990. Estudio Actual de la Vegetación de la cordillera Chongón Colonche. Instituto de Investigación de Recursos Naturales. Facultad de Ciencias Naturales.

Valverde, Flor de María; Patricia Choez & Camilo Reyes 2004. «Situación de la biodiversidad en las Albarradas y sectores colindantes de la planicie costera de las provincias de Guayas y Manabí», en: Marcos J.G. (coord.) *Albarradas en la Costa del Ecuador: Rescate del Conocimiento Ancestral del Manejo Sostenible de la Biodiversidad.* CEAA-ESPOL, Guayaquil, Ecuador.

Water Management in Ancient Ecuador

Jorge G. Marcos

Abstract

Early societies in Ancient Ecuador developed in tune with the Holocene mega diversity that characterized the area since 7800 BC. After a long Paleo-Indian (*Upper Palaeolithic*) mode of living (c. 11 000 – 8500 BC.) followed by the Archaic *or Neolithic Pre-ceramic* (8500–4000 BC.), the raise of the Formative Period *[Neolithic]* took place with the introduction of ceramic manufacture (3900 BC.) and the modification of the environment into a productive landscape. Important elements in the modification of the ecosystem to secure more stable production were constructions destined to manage rainfall, especially flooding (raised fields) and the runoff (Albarradas), in areas where: 1. The floodplain remains under water a good part of the year and, 2. Rainfall is low most of the year with uncertain seasons of intensive rains. Other system to harvest drinking water was to condense fogs from the cloud forest in the coastal cordilleras of the Santa Elena Peninsula and Southern Manabí. In this paper such systems are described and discussed.

Introduction

During the past three decades our research has focused on the environmental changes in coastal Ecuador produced both by climate change and by human interaction with the natural environment. The highly diversified landscape of the Holocene permitted foragers from the archaic period to settle and begin to produce plant foods and create basic planting, harvesting and food processing tools; in their endeavor they cemented relationships with hunter gatherers who collected in the mangrove stands, fished the intertidal and the open sea, they also traded with people who mined the hard rocks needed to produce axe heads, creating complex networks of exchange. The highly diversified equatorial landscape generated trade relationships with other early farming groups which allowed them to settle and in time begin making ceramic vessels. This changes in production occurred some two thousand years earlier than in Mesoamerica or in the Central Andes. But more important, these farmers began to generate an anthropogenic environment transforming the natural landscape as they build villages, pathways, roads, causeways to communicate between urban centers, also constructed walls, and planted gardens and fields. As agriculture became their main form of production they began to generate astronomical and calendrical sightlines in order to organize planting and harvesting. To intensify production they built water management systems, organized social complexity by creating ceremonial centers with mounds that supported religious and political structures and wishing and predictive rites to request and control the amount and intensity of rains.

Equatorial South America's environment at the end of the Glacial Optimum

Since the 1980's scientists have been debating whether the Amazonian lowlands were significantly drier during Pleistocene glacial maxima or colder or both, and whether or not the Amazon forest was reduced to a few *Pleistocene refuges* with consequent effects on present-day diversity and endemism patterns of plants and animals in the Neotropical lowlands (Whitmore and Prance, 1987).

When the first Paleo-Indian hunter-gatherers arrived to equatorial South America at the end of the glacial optimum (13 000–8000 BC.), they found that climate was probably cooler than it is today, probably 5–7°C cooler, and also somewhat drier, with perhaps 25–40% less rainfall than at present. Bio-scientific research suggests that the Orinoco and Amazonian lowlands, as well as the lowlands of the Guayas Basin were covered in those days by large patches of savanna, while forests clung to the upper Amazon, the foothills at both sides of the Andes, and the Guyana and Brazilian upper plain, and the tropical rivers were festooned by gallery forests (Whitmore and Prance, 1987:1–45). The great rivers did not carry as much water as they do today, for most of the water was frozen in the glaciers, and the sea level was 130 m. below its present mark. This made the lowlands both sides of the Andes, an ideal habitat for hunter gatherers of the Pleistocene Megafauna.

The grasslands and scattered forests at the Orinoco Llanos, the Amazon basin, coastal Ecuador and the extreme north coast of Peru were host to *Mastodons*, giant sloth (*Megatherium* and *Mylodon*), the sabre-toothed tiger (*Smilodon*), the giant armadillos (*Glyptodont*), the giant llama (*Paleolama*), etc., and were thriving when the diverse bands of hunting gatherers arrived there after 15 000 BC. It was in this setting that a distinct equatorial Paleo-Indian mode of living developed.

The hunter-gatherers of the Pleistocene Period were fulltime searchers for plants to eat, and for animals to hunt. During this time they developed and array of stone, bone and shell tools to aid them in hunting, fishing and to collect and process the plants they gathered for food and fibers. They also were great travelers. It appears that their ability to adapt to changing environments and resources was one their most important survival assets. However, we should consider that some of these changes in environment and diet occurred in longer periods than the lifespan of a single individual, and that some of their more distant journeys probably took more than one or two generations. Therefore their survival ability was that of populations rather than of individuals.

The raise of Agriculture

Some ten thousand years ago agriculture was already supplying part of the diet to the people of the Neotropics. Archaeologists, as a general concept, suggest that plant domestication began because of rising populations. Because of agriculture's ability to provide a stable and large quantity of produce, population densities then grew even more.

However, this process was more complex, especially in areas of the equatorial tropics, where the Holocene climate change was responsible not only for reducing the savanna and increasing the forests cover, but also for creating a myriad of environments. The territories occupied by Ecuador today became one of the mega diverse environments in the World. It was this patchwork of microenvironments that permitted early settlements and set the base for the process of neolitization that resulted in the Valdivia culture sites of coastal Ecuador.

Plants became a major factor during this period as well. The early use of plants gave rise to weeds; these appear to be the result of human interaction with the environment. From Mesoamerica to South America pimentos [chillies and aji] (*Capsicum spp.*), squash or pumpkin (*Curcubita maxima, C, pepo*), beans (*Phaseolus spp.*), quinoa (*Chenopodium quinoa*), peanuts (*Arachis hypogaea*), manioc (*Manihot spp.*), achira (*Canna edulis*), and other tubers were well on their way to being domesticated a few thousand years before the first permanent communities appeared. Possibly earlier than that, Teosintle (*Zea americana*), the apparent ancestor of corn (*Zea maize*) (Beadle 1977, 1980), was already a weed, the camp follower of hunter-gatherers during the late Paleo-Indian Period. Corn, the unviable mutation of Teosintle, subsisted only by human intervention, coevolving with mankind the following millennia. Apparently, maize was a component of the early dooryard garden of the late foragers that inhabited Mesoamerica and northern South America. According to Piperno (1990), maize phytoliths are present at the corings taken from the ancient shores of Lake *Ayauch* in south-eastern Ecuador, dating to c. 6000 BC (7000 BP), and the presence of charcoal bits associated with maize phytoliths suggest to Piperno the use of slash-and-burn to plant maize plots around 4200 BC (5300 BP.).

From Dooryard Garden to Productive Landscape

Early societies in Ancient Ecuador developed in tune within a changing environment, the Holocene mega diversity that characterized the area since 7800 BC. After a long Paleo-Indian (*Upper Palaeolithic*) mode of living (c. 11 000 – 8500 BC.) followed by the Archaic *or Neolithic Pre-ceramic* (8500–4000 BC.).

The raise of the Formative Period *[Neolithic]* began with the introduction of ceramic manufacture (3900 BC.) and the modification of the environment into a productive landscape. The process of neolitization implied not only the exploitation and management of the mega diverse equatorial landscape formed by a great number of varied micro-environments. It also meant the development of exchange networks of wide-ranging products, and conquering rivers for trade.

Controlling river basins from the flood plain up the foothills, and to the hilltops, as landscape modifying technologies were developed, and their introduction permitted to manage the landscape and to increase production. This co-evolutionary process began when the first hunter gatherers started modifying the landscape with the use of fire, and manipulating useful plants which they planted near their shelters. From this period onwards, and for a good time to come, the shelters and planting fields of the first farmers were close to water sources and near the floodplains of the fluvial systems.

Water management of Rivers and their Flood Plain

The best example of extensive agriculture in ancient Ecuador comes from the Guayas Basin, at the *Perinao* site, north of *Colimes de Balzar*. The excavation of the remnants of a Valdivia Period temporary shack dating from c. 3300 BC (4510+100 BP, ISGS-478A; 4460+100 BP, ISGS-478B) on the left bank of an olden river meander of the Daule River gave evidence of plantings on the river bank and levee (Raymond, Marcos and Lathrap, 1983, Ziólkowski, et.al. 1994: 149).

Fig. 1 Excavation on the left bank of the Daule River at Perinao

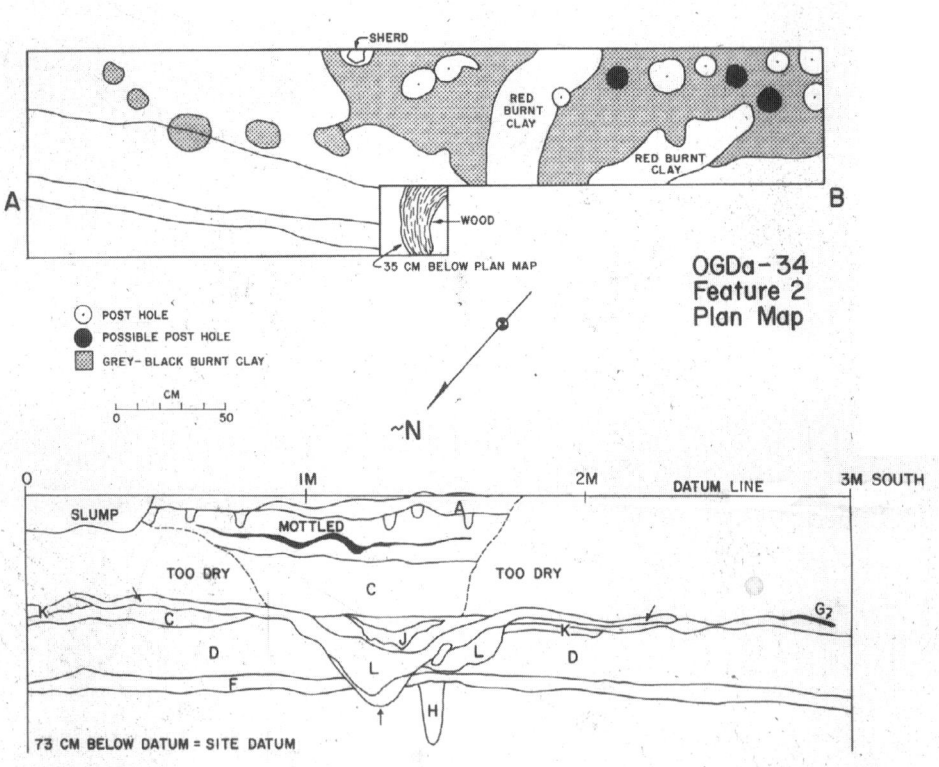

X-section of Feature 2

Besides the dates (above) diagnostic Valdivia 2a shards were found on the structure floor (see below).

Fig. 2: The excavation of Feature 2 on the ancient Daule River bank at Perinao

Ethnographic observation of traditional river banks extensive agriculture in the Guayas Basin riverine system, and archaeological data, permitted the reconstruction of the manner this site functioned.

The rainy season in the Guayas Basin comes to an end in the month of May. Then the tropical rivers reduce their flow and the water level begins to drop slowly, until they become a mere trickle by November or December, when it begins to rain again. During this period farmers do extensive dry season planting on the expose river channel.

The top of the natural levee is covered by large shade trees dominated by Palo prieto (*Eritrina spp.*), and Samán (*Samanea saman*) and below their canopy, cacao and coffee alternate with mangoes (*Mangifera indica* L), breadfruit (*Artocarpus altilis* (Parkinson) (Fosberg), and the dooryard plants commonly planted at the beginning of the rainy season once the rivers have overflowed the levee and spilled into the flood plain beyond, covering it.

Guayas basin farmers follow a time honoured planting schedule on the river bank, as the waters recede they plant, just below the top of the levee: manioc (*Manihot esculenta*, Cranz), sweet potato (*Ipomoea batata*, L.), and other plants that need more than four to five months to mature. Immediately below, in perpendicular rows to the river channel, they alternate corn (*Zea mais.* L.), tobacco (*Nicotine tobacum*, L.) with beans (*Phaseolus vulgaris* L.); below this, they plant patches of gourds (*Lagenaria siceraria*), pumpkins (*Curcubita maxima* and *C. pepo*), squash (*Cucurbita moschata* Duch.) melons (*Cucumis melo* L.) and watermelons (*Citrullus lanatus*). Finally, between July and August, when the water level is at ebb, peanuts (*Arachis hypogaea*) above the water line and below the peanuts, on the waterline they now plant rice (*Oryza sativa*). Before they begin the planting schedule, farmers built a temporary shelter similar to the remnants found at the Perinao site. The location of the archaeological remnants of a temporary hut that had burnt to the ground and the charred foot of the main post allowed dating it to 3300 BC, which is 600 years before extensive agriculture appeared at Real Alto, suggesting the tropical forested Guayas Basin was the loci for the development of more complex forms of Valdivia agriculture.

After approximately one thousand three hundred years, farmers began making considerable modifications on the landscape to increase production and to save and manage rain water. They began building Raised Fields in the lower Guayas Basin and Albarradas or *Jagüeyes* in the Santa Elena Peninsula.

Camellones: Raised or Ridged Fields

The floodplain of the lower Guayas Basin covers approximately 90,000 hectares, and remains under water roughly six months out of the year. At least 42,000 hectares were transformed in pre-Columbian times for year around production through the construction of raised field or 'Camellones'. According to Parsons and Schlemon (1987) radiocarbon dating of organic sediments excavated in the channels of raised fields built north of Duran, across the river from Guayaquil demonstrated that these were in use at about 2000 BC. Camellones or raised fields are an anthropogenic system which converts large tracks of wetlands into a productive landscape. This was achieved by the excavation of parallel channels (artificial river) separated by mounded banks created by depositing the material excavated from the artificial channel at one side. The artificial banks kept above the water level during the monsoon permitted year around agriculture (maize, manioc, beans, squash and cacao; while the channels were used for aquiculture: fishes, mussels, crabs, turtles and waterfowl prospered in and around them. During the dry season also attracted game, crocodiles and caimans the latter were purported to have kept the channels free of heavy sedimentation. Experimental research (Muse and Quintero 1987) showed ridged fields to have been a very efficient and economically successful system.

Jagüeyes[6] or Albarradas[7]

About the same time that the first Camellones were being built in the lower Guayas Basin (c. 2000 BC) the natives of the Santa Elena Peninsula began building detention ponds (*Jagüeyes* or *Albarradas*) to contain the runoff, stop the washing out of the topsoil and let the water percolate into de underlying Pleistocene sandstone fossil beaches of the Tablazo Formation, thus recharging the subsurface aquifer

In 1998 the author presented a project proposal to the Global Environmental Facility GEF, in Washington DC., a «block A» to prepare a Mid-Size Project was granted him in 1999, later that same year the GEF-World Bank approved the Project, the author was named General Coordinator of the Project and Escuela Superior Politecnica del Litoral ESPOL the recipient partner of the grant, secured other project partners like NASA's Rapid Rate of Change Project lead by Hector D'Antoni.

---

6. Variants of term *Jagüey* (apparently of Quechua origin) are used today in the Americas, *Jagüey* from Mexico to Colombia, *Jaguay* or *Jaguei* in Peru or *Jagüel* in Argentina. It is considered in Argentina that the word *jagüel* «derives from the Quechua *jagüei* or *jagüey* and it means a well or a ditch that receives and conserves rainwater from the runoff or form a natural spring.»
7. *Albarradas* is the name by which *Jagüeyes* are known in Ecuador since the beginning of the 20th Century, and apparently refers to its horseshoe-shape detention wall. The term *Albarrada* it is normally used to refer to a wall built by an earth embankment. The Collins Spanish-English dictionary (1971) indicates that in the Andes it also means *Cistern*.

The Albarradas Project main objective was to rescue knowledge of the traditional sustainable management of biodiversity and fresh water resources in a region where fresh water supply is a critical problem, especially for the extreme poor. The Project was executed by ESPOL's Center for Archeological and Anthropological Research and supported by the Global Environmental Facility GEF, the World Bank.

Charcoal samples assessment by the Radiocarbon Laboratory of the University of Arizona (Tucson), was financed by the Project *Rapid Rates of Change* of the Ames Research Centre at NASA, the results show that the *Albarradas system* is the result of a long–term process. The earliest were built during terminal Valdivia (c. 1,800 BC); at Muey during Machalilla and Engoroy phases (1,500 – 300 BC), and continued to be built and rebuilt the Huancavilca society (AD 900 – AD 1500).

The project objectives were met by multidisciplinary research, different research teams discussed the implications of their findings in relation to the objectives and indicators, validating them, and/or generating new hypothesis, when needed, to further refine and test variations of the initial research hypothesis and indicators. All specific research hypotheses were tested and validated by the different research teams, the results have been beyond the project initial expectations.

El Niño

The advances of warm water produce seasonal rains in south west Ecuador and in northern Peru, this phenomenon linked to the «El Niño Southern Oscillation» (ENSO). The climate of this area is characterized by the northern-most influence of the Humboldt Current, which is expected to give way to advances of the warm waters from the warm Panamanian current from December to May. The rivers in the area are dry most of the year. When it rains, during a normal rainy season, they can flood for a short time, and then they run a trickle of water until the next rain. Rains can be totally absent for several years, but when hard seasonal rains, or an El Niño event occur, most of the water from the run-off is lost into the sea.

In the pre-Columbian past, the people of the Santa Elena Peninsula developed adaptive strategies in the face ENSO events. Around 2000 BC they began building detention ponds (*Jagüeyes* or *Albarradas*) to contain the runoff and to stop the washing out of the topsoil. These detention ponds allowed rainwater to percolate into the underlying Pleistocene sandstone fossil beaches thus recharging the subsurface aquifer of the Tablazo Formation. (Tablazo Formation is the raised Pleistocene beaches which left a finely porous sandstone substrate, which is found along the Pacific coast of Ecuador and northern Peru) (Bristow and Hoffstetter, 1977).

Figure 3 depicts the ways Albarradas are constructed: The horseshoe-shaped earth embankments (7) built around a borrow pit and placed with 'arms' (8) open, facing the incline (5) to trap rainwater from the runoff. One of the main purposes for building the Albarradas was to trap water from the runoff and allow it to sink into the aquifer (3) of the Tablazo Formation (4), which was later extracted from wells excavated in the center (1) or to one side of the Albarrada embankment (2). The Albarrada overflow was always built on the natural drainage (11). Albarradas are surrounded by the dry forest and shrubs stands (9), and near the center of the Commune (10).

Fig. 3 Albarrada System diagram Taken from Marcos 2004:329

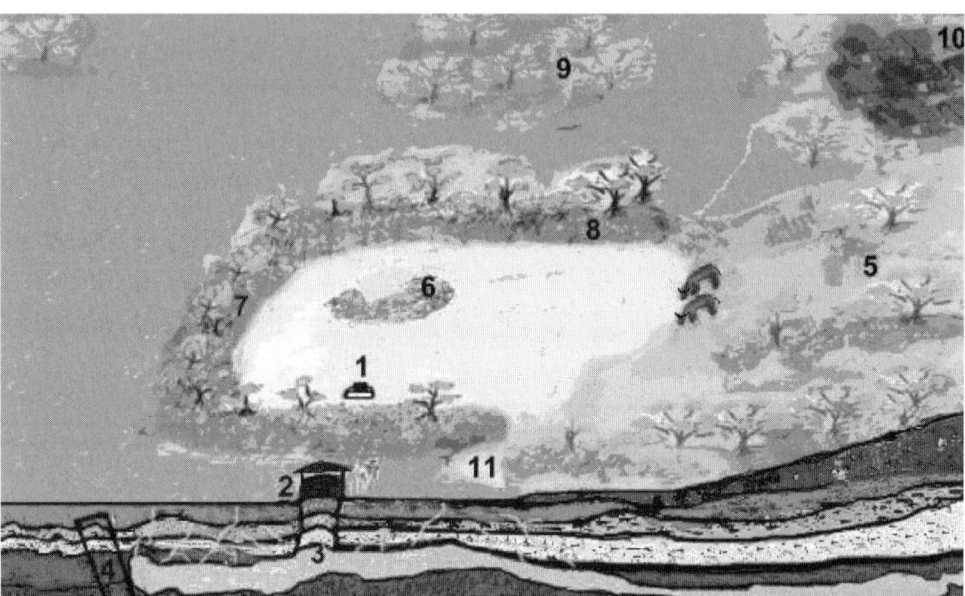

Muey is an ancient settlement in the point of Santa Elena between La Libertad and Salinas, more that two hundred Albarradas were built in this relatively small area. Today only seven large and complex systems of Albarradas still survive in Muey. What makes the Muey system unique is that around 850 BC the ancient inhabitants of the area excavated sunken fields in the middle of an area covered by nearly 250 small detention ponds. Their excavation reached almost to the water table, and planted on the humidified sunken surface. The people from Muey had created sunken garden agriculture, an agricultural system that was further developed in ancient Peru. Another important reason for Albarradas construction was to secure drinking water, a scarce element in a semidry region. Agustín de Zárate[8], one of the chroniclers of the Conquest of Peru, wrote in 1555 that 'this land is very dry, although it rains often; there runs little fresh water (the rivers run dry), and everyone drinks from wells or from detention ponds which the natives call *Jagüeyes*.'

The Albarradas Project Results

The project resulted in the identification of 8 wild botanical species relatives of the crop varieties and ancient cultivars plus 31 endemic species and 180 species registered as endemic for the Galapagos Islands, showing that the Albarradas system aids to the conservation and sustainable use of dry tropical forests. This has been confirmed by socio-

---

8. Zárate, Agustín de *Historia del Descubrimiento y Conquista del Perú*. Edition, notes and preliminary study by Franklin Pease G.Y. and Teodoro Hampe Martínez, Colección Clásicos Peruanos, Lima, Pontificia Universidad Católica del Perú, Editorial Fund 1995.

cultural analysis which has determined and rescued the knowledge of indigenous people, improving our understanding of sustainability issues in biodiversity.

Important aspects of traditional Albarrada construction have been determined: site selection, natural drainage, wall construction in thin deposit layers of sequential sediments extracted from central borrow pits that accounts for a strong horseshoe-shaped wall. The Albarradas project data base is essential to understand traditional adaptive strategies, because it shows how the ancestors of the present native populations developed a system to take advantage of the positive aspects of El Niño events, as well as to ameliorate its negative impacts on biodiversity and society. Albarradas in Ecuador and Wachaques (a combination detention pond and sunken garden) in northern Peru are still maintained today by the native communities that live in the area (Marcos, 2004).

Water management of the hilltops (cloud-forest)

Until the end of the late Formative Period (c. 300 BC) the area of appropriation and modification of the environment in coastal valleys was for the most part the valley bottom, from the riverine floodplain to the 70 meter contour line. During the Regional Developmental Period (c. 100 BC – AD 800) the Guangala people of the Santa Elena Peninsula began terracing the foothills and by AD 900 the Manteño-Huancavilca society terraced the coastal cordilleras all the way to the hilltops. To obtain drinking water they developed a water capturing system to condense water from the fogs of the cloud forest (Marcos, 1995:142–48). The «Camanchaca» Project), supported by ROSTA-LAC/UNESCO/PNUD allowed us to study the pre-Columbian fog (*Camanchaca*) water condensing systems developed since AD 700 in the cloud-forest of the Chogón-Colonche cordillera from 1984 to 1987.

Agricultural terracing occurs at the Chogón-Colonche cordillera, the cordilleras of the Manabí basin, and the coastal cordilleras like the Chanduy hills and at Azucar. Elements of the water-condensing systems have been observed by Zevallos in Juntas (1934), and by Tobar and Álvarez along the Chogón-Colonche cordillera and in the Chanduy hills (Marcos, 1995), and by Masucci at Azucar.

The geology of the cordilleras of the central and south-western Ecuadorian coast is very complex[9]. To archaeologists working in the area are of special interest the conglomerates, pebbly sandstones, sandstones, shale and the Holocene clay and gravel conglomerates that cover the foothills of the Chogón-Colonche Cordillera, the Chanduy and Cabras Hills (Bristow and Hoffstetter, 1977). It is precisely on this hard-to-penetrate surface that hill farmers began building a cloud forest water condensing systems around AD 700.

The system consisted of hillside terracing for planting maize, parabolic flagstone-lined pools, on hill-top mesas to collect the condensed fog «rain». These pools were surrounded by planted trees covered by different kinds of bromeliads which acted like condensers and extracted water from the cloud. From the pools, drain-trenches carried water to stone-lined cylindrical cisterns 0.6 meters in diameter and 1.5 meters deep, dug at one side of the agricultural terraces. Below the terraces, on the foothills, several granaries conserved the harvested maize.

In order to anchor the granaries and keep them off the ground, early Manteño-Huancavilca farmers used isosceles triangular stones which they drove apex-down into the ground, the triangle base was grooved to anchor the wattle and daub platform-floor that supported the granary. Similar granaries are still used in Bolivia; the difference is the short pillars which support the granary platform are made of wood, while the pre-Columbian ones from Ecuador were placed on stone cleaves, which were able to penetrate the hard-to-dig gravel-clay conglomerate.

The three systems discussed shows the inventive know-how of the pre-Columbian farmers of ancient Ecuador and their in tune with nature development, it also permits to understand the devastating impact, that during the last 500 years, the productive landscape these ancient farmers built has been subjected to.

---

9. The Cayo Formation crops out on both sides of the Chongon-Colonche fault. The Cayo Formation was mainly deposited in a shallow-marine environment with west-directed transport. Conformable contacts with underlying fine-grained deposits of the Calentura Formation indicate that an important tectonic and geodynamic change occurred by Late Cretaceous (late Coniacian-early Santonian) time. The Santa Elena Formation is pelagic black chert and tuff; probable reservoirs are marine sandstones. Deposition of the Santa Elena Formation was followed by substantial tectonic subsidence that accommodated thick, uppermost Paleocene turbidites of the Azucar Group. The upper Paleocene to lower Eocene Azucar Group is only located south of the Chongon- Colonche fault and is composed of at least 1,500 m (5,000 ft) of conglomerates, pebbly sandstones, sandstones, and shales (Bristow and Hoffstetter, 1977) that form reservoirs and seals. Direction of the paleocurrent was from the northeast; the Azucar Group is faulted and contains east, northeast-to-west-, and southwest-trending folds with vertical axial planes. Sediments were deposited on submarine fans largely by high-density (with minor low-density) turbidite flows. Source of sediments are the underlying Santa Elena and Guayaquil Formations (lateral equivalent in the Chongon-Colonche Cordillera) and continental basement and volcanic. The Azucar Group is unconformably overlain by the lower Eocene El Rosario Formation. The Quaternary La Cruz Formation is greenish-gray shale with benthonic and planktonic foraminifera of sublittoral depositional environments, and the Quaternary Tablazo Formation is primarily marine coquinas, sand, and gravel.

Bibliography

Álvarez, Silvia

1988 Recuperación y defensa de territorio étnico en la Costa ecuatoriana: el caso de la Antigua Comunidad de Indígenas de Chanduy, en: Hombre y Ambiente, el Punto de Vista Indígena (8): Abya-Yala, Quito.

1991 Los Comuneros de Santa Elena. Tierra, Familia y Propiedad. Biblioteca de Ciencias Sociales Vol. 34, Corporación Editorial Nacional, Abya-Yala, Quito.

Álvarez, Silvia; Martín Bazurco; Mónica Burmester y Claudia González Andricaín 2004. «Organización social, cultura y gestión de los Sistemas de Albarradas en la PSE», en: Marcos J.G. (coord.) *Albarradas en la Costa del Ecuador: Rescate del Conocimiento Ancestral del Manejo Sostenible de la Biodiversidad.* CEAA-ESPOL, Guayaquil, Ecuador.

Beadle, G. W., 1980 The ancestry of corn. *Scientific American* 242: 112–119.

Beadle, G. W., 1977 The origin of Zea mays, pp. 615–635 in *Origins of Agriculture,* edited by C. A. Reed. Mouton Press, The Hague.

Bristow, C. R. y Hoffsteter, Robert 1973 Ecuador (Equateur) Amérique Latine, fascicule 5 a 2, *Lexique Statighraphique,* Union Internationale des Sciences Geologiques, Paris.

Centro de Promoción Rural 1990 (MS) Documento Preliminar sobre el Diagnóstico socio-económico de las Comunas en la Dinámica Peninsular, 53 pp., Guayaquil, Ecuador.

Hoffstetter, Robert. 1956: Lexique stratigraphique international. Amérique latine: Ecuador. Congreso Geológico Internacional de México, 5/5a, 191 p.

Lanning, Edward P. 1964 Informe Preliminar de la Península de Santa Elena. Presentado a la Casa de la Cultura Ecuatoriana.

Leff, Enrique 1998 Saber Ambiental, Sustentabilidad, Racionalidad, Complejidad, Poder. Siglo XXI. México.

McDougle, Eugene 1967 Water use and Settlements in Changing Environments of the Southern Ecuadorian Coast. Submitted in Partial Fulfillment of the Requirements for the Degree of Master of Art, in the Faculty of Political Science, Columbia University.

Marcos, Jorge G. 1995 El Manejo del Agua en el Variado Medioambiente del Área Septentrional Andina a Partir del Tercer Milenio B.C., en Actas del Simposio Cultura y Medioambiente en el Área *Septentrional Andina* (M. Guinea,].F. Bouchard y].G. Marcos, eds.), pp. 127–164. Editores Abya Yala, Quito.

Marcos, Jorge G. (coord..) *Albarradas en la costa del Ecuador: Rescate del Conocimiento Ancestral del Manejo Sostenible de la Biodiversidad.* CEAA-ESPOL, Guayaquil, Ecuador.

Marcos, Jorge G. y Oswaldo Tobar 2004 «La investigación arqueológica e histórica de las Albarradas de la Costa», en: Marcos J.G. (coord.) *Albarradas en la Costa del Ecuador: Rescate del Conocimiento Ancestral del Manejo Sostenible de la Biodiversidad.* CEAA-ESPOL, Guayaquil, Ecuador.

Marcos, Jorge G. & Martín Bazurco 2006 «Albarradas y Camellones en la región costera del Antiguo Ecuador» En. *Agricultura Ancestral. Camellones y Albarradas: Contexto social, usos y retos del pasado y del presente.* Pp.93–110. Ediciones Abya-

Yala / IFEA / IRD / Banco Central del Ecuador / INPC / CNRS / Embajada de Francia en Ecuador / Universidad París I

Muse, Michael and Quintero, Fausto 1987 Experimentos de reactivación de campos elevados, Peñón del Río, Guayas, Ecuador. *BAR. International Series* 359(ii):249–267.

Parsons, James J.; Roy Schlemon 1987 Mapping and dating the Prehistoric Raised Fields of the Guayas Basin, Ecuador. Simposio Pre Hispanic Agricultural Fields in the Andean region, Part II. W. Denevan, K Mathewson, and G. Knapp. Proceedings 45° Congreso Internacional de Americanistas, Bogotá, Colombia 1985. Bar International Series 359 (II): 217–224.

Piperno, Dolores. 1990 Aboriginal agriculture and land usage in the Amazon basin, Ecuador, *Journal of Archaeological Science* 17, 665- 6

Raymond, J. Scott, Jorge G. Marcos and Donald W. Lathrap 1983 Evidence of Early Formative Settlement in the Guayas Basin, Ecuador: *Current Anthropology* 21, H.5: 700–701.

Stothert, Karen 1995 Las Albarradas tradicionales y el manejo de aguas en la Península de Santa Elena, en: Miscelánea Antropológica ecuatoriana, Boletín del Área Cultural del Banco Central del Ecuador, 8:131–160, Guayaquil, Ecuador.

Valverde, Flor de María; GR. Tazán y C. García 1979 Cubierta Vegetal en la Península de Santa Elena. Facultad de Ciencias Naturales. Universidad de Guayaquil.

Valverde, Flor de María; G. Rodríguez y C. García 1991 Estudio Actual de la Vegetación de la cordillera Chongón Colonche. Instituto de Investigación de Recursos Naturales. Facultad de Ciencias Naturales.

Valverde, Flor de María; Patricia Choez & Camilo Reyes 2004 «Situación de la biodiversidad en las Albarradas y sectores colindantes de la planicie costera de las provincias de Guayas y Manabí», en: Marcos J.G. (coord.) *Albarradas en la Costa del Ecuador: Rescate del Conocimiento Ancestral del Manejo Sostenible de la Biodiversidad*. CEAA-ESPOL, Guayaquil, Ecuador.

Whitmore, T.C. & G. T. Prance, eds. 1987 *Biogeography and Quaternary History in Tropical America*, Oxford Monographs in Biogeography N°3, Oxford: Clarendon Press.

Zárate, Agustín de 1995 *Historia del Descubrimiento y Conquista del Perú*. Edición, notas y estudio preliminar por Franklin Pease G.Y. y Teodoro Hampe Martínez. Colección Clásicos Peruanos, Pontificia Universidad Católica del Perú, Fondo Editorial, Lima

Zevallos Menéndez, Carlos 1934 Postes totémicos en la Cordillera Chongón Colonche. Revista Cultura, *Diario El Telégrafo*, Guayaquil.

Ziólkowski, M.S., M. F. Pazdur, A. Krzanowski, A. Michczynski, 1994 *ANDES – Radiocarbon Database for Bolivia, Ecuador and Perú*, Joint publication – Andean Archaeological Mission of the Institute of Archaeology, Warsaw University & Gliwice Radiocarbon Laboratory of the Institute of Physics, Silesian Technical University, Warszawa – Giwice.

The Use and Traditional Knowledge of Pre-Hispanic Hydraulic Systems amongst Indigenous and Non-Indigenous Populations on the Ecuadorian Coast

Silvia G. Álvarez[10]

Introduction

In the Ecuadorian coastal region several pre-Columbian hydraulic systems (Detention Ponds [*Albarradas or Jagüeyes*] and Raised Fields [*Campos de Camellones*]) coexist[11] today. Their origin dates back to around the same period (ca. 2000B.C.) and represents adaptations to regional environmental conditions: raised fields were made to control an excess of water during the rainy season, and albarradas were built to respond to cyclical water shortages (Marcos 1987, 1995). At present, the villagers in some settlements located in these areas acknowledge these hydraulic systems as part of their indigenous past and identify with them; whilst others do not mention it at all. Indeed, when the villagers' relations with the ancient water management systems are compared, varying attitudes and values can be discerned.

In the lower Guayas Basin, more than 40.000 hectares of land modified for raised fields has been registered since the 1960's (Denevan, Mathewson and Knapp 1987). Although these studies in archaeology and cultural ecology clearly document the complexity of these hydraulic systems, the people living in the region today ignore their origin and potential, and do not relate to them as part of their indigenous heritage (Álvarez 1987, 1989).

In contrast, most of the villages organized in communes on the Ecuadorian coast acknowledge albarradas (detention ponds) systems as structures and physical resourc-

---

10. Coordinator of the Albarradas Project socio-cultural team, 2000-2003; the team included Yolanda Gutiérrez, Koën Peteers, Mónica Burmester, Martín Bazurco, Claudia González, Pía Escobar and Oscar Arias.
11. i.e. raised fields [*campos de camellones*], and detention ponds [*albarradas or Jagüeyes*]).

es as a heritage endowed them by their indigenous ancestors (Marcos 2004). However, when these traditional detention ponds systems are managed by others than the natives that live in communal lands because now some of the traditional territory has been appropriated by local government (parishes and cantons) the level of information about the origin, potential and use modes of Albarradas changes considerably. There the population identifies mainly as mestizo, and their knowledge about traditional albarradas is remote or non existent. Although private property has been introduced in territories occupied by local governments the mestizo population in this area still use and maintain the detention ponds as collective property which they can all use freely[12]. This is illustrated by *Paján Canton, Julcuy Parish* (Province of Manabí), *Valle de la Virgen Parish, El Morro Parish* and *Ayalán Hacienda* [country estate] (Province of Guayas where the inhabitants, in diverse senses and at a different level of awareness, acknowledge and value the significance of the Albarradas and the role they play.

In this paper our aim is to ponder the loss of connection shown by some present day local farmers with pre-Colonial hydraulic systems technologies. We interpret this loss as the outcome of a replacement and devaluation of this native heritage in response to the changing power relations forced on them beginning during the Colonial period and continuing until today. The subordinated condition which the indigenous population has been placed also generates an image laden with prejudices towards their cultural products and among them their traditional technological advances. This image is also sustained by institutions and individuals with University level educations, who discard these systems from their usual research programmes; the result being that indigenous perspectives rarely appear in development project designs. This situation is highlighted by Claudia Gonzalez (this volume) when she shows how asymmetrical relations between local knowledge and scientific knowledge impinge on the sustainability of these traditional hydraulic systems.

The current use of raised fields in the Cuenca del Guayas [Guayas Basin]

The «Peñón-del-Río» Project supported by a USAID Science department grant (1980–1986), fostered multidisciplinary research on raised fields or *campos de camellones* in the lower Guayas river basin (Marcos this volume; Marcos,1987; Marcos and Bazurco 2005). The socio-cultural research carried out by the project demonstrated that most interviewed peasants working in agriculture, fishing, or as landless labourers, did not identify with the system. Their testimonies attributed the existence of the «Camellones[13]» or raised fields to divine or natural creation: «*God made them,*» or «*they were made by nature*». This last interpretation also dominated scientific discourses until cul-

---

12. However, when these same systems are administered by non-communal organizations (*parroquias* and *cantones*), where most people self-identify as mestizo [mixed white and Indigenous blood], their recognition of the the detention ponds' origin, potential and mode of usage is, however, quite different.
13. Camellones or raised fields are built by excavating channels on the surface of seasonal wetlands and placing the excavated deposit to one side of the channel, to raise the level of planting surfaces. When several (parallel) channels are dug an equal number of elevated of (parallel) planting surface cover the area, permitting year around planting and harvesting. The channels are used to keep domestic water foul and other forms of aquiculture.

tural geography proved that they were aboriginal constructions; their main role being landscape modification of land that inundates during the rainy season or El Niño events and to ease a second harvest during summer. Study also revealed that they were periodically maintained to improve soil fertility (Parsons and Shlemon, 1987).

The region was reoccupied during the Colonial period by a mixed population of outsiders (Europeans, African slaves, Indigenous people from the *Sierra* [Andean valleys]) who cornered and dispossessed of land and the remnants of the region's original inhabitants. This new population introduced major changes to the existing resource-use and management-patterns of raised-fields. A change that explains the extensive damage inflicted to the *Camellones* system at this point in time.

After the sixteenth century the lower Guayas Basin Indian territories were divided and turned into private property through the Spanish introduction of the hacienda system, and a plantation model that destined production for export. Initially used for cattle or cacao production, the existing system of raised fields played a major role in the production of these commodities. The shift to rice production and agricultural mechanization during the Second World War, however, made the raised fields obsolete. The recent introduction of freshwater shrimp farming into the area has further intensified their destruction (Álvarez, 1990). Permanently mobile and serving the new economy as a manual labour force, the population lost its ties to the pre-Colonial productive system. Consequently, people lost both their power to decide on natural resources, and their knowledge and management skills of what once had been local cultural heritage. This patrimony was substituted or marginalized when it failed to meet the objectives set by the goals of the new projects of the capitalist market started in the colonial period.

At present, there are few areas where this hydraulic system remains intact. In those areas where it still exists, the original use of the system has been modified beyond recognition. An analysis carried out by the Albarradas Project's socio-cultural studies team in twenty rice cooperatives of the region shows that only a few small farmers continue to use raised fields in the same integrated and complex manner they were designed to be used when created by native farmers during the pre-Columbian period. Some farmers conserve raised fields in their land to protect their homes, household garden and rice paddies from the rising water level during the rainy season, i.e. «*Camellones serve to prevent seedlings* (rice) *from drowning*» (Álvarez 1989).

It is however, when the El Niño[14] events occur, that these systems become of vital importance. In addition to keeping crops and animals above the rising water, they also save houses from destruction. Local houses built on top of the raised platforms of the ridged fields are kept above the flood which turns the countryside into a humid wasteland for more than six months of the year.

During regular precipitations in non-El Niño years, the Santa Elena and especially the lower Guayas river basin are unreachable by dirt-roads during the rainy season, these roads being turned into mud puddles. The only means of transport during this season is by riverboat, motor canoe and other means of fluvial transport. In short, the only places that remain above the flood are the top of the raised fields called by local

---

14. El Niño is a disruption of the ocean-atmosphere system in the Tropical Pacific having important consequences for weather and climate around the globe

farmers «*lomas*» (hillocks). It is during these periods that the population thanks providence and their ancestors for leaving this high terrain, an adaptive resource built to survive the climate changes that continue to seasonally condition life in the humid equatorial lowlands.

Despite their value, however, few present day farmers preserve, replicate or maintain these *Camellones*. Indeed, local farmers in general failed to organize or carry put the collective work needed to mend or protect them. On a daily basis, the local population does not feel part of this cultural landscape, and has –in the past two to three hundred years– cleared the terrain of trees to work the land for market-oriented production. Thes cooperative farmers who obtain economic benefit from these raised fields do nothing to increase the technological capacity of these fields. Nor is there any evidence of their trying to reproduce them, because the principles and rationale underlying the original raised fields' have been lost or are ignored. As a result of the fact, that before the Agrarian Reform decreed in (Decree 1001), rural (manual) labour land was legally defined as precarious (land held as a loan for labour such as forest clearing or share cropping), farm working families remained and made use of the land at the pleasure of the owner of the expanded agricultural frontier. This meant that ancient technologies were practically abandoned. Migration, especially among men, and the type of matriarchal family that ensued, also undoubtedly influenced the transmission of the traditional knowledge of how to successfully manage the raised-fields system (Álvarez, 1989).

The Peñón del Rio Project's multidisciplinary efforts helped to bracketed together the archaeological, agronomic, and socio-cultural expertise needed for two agronomic experiments on raised fields (1983 and 1984). These experiments sought to update the multiple uses of raised fields, and communicate the system's qualities to the people who currently occupy the fields. It was the first time in Ecuador that experiments were carried out on this hydraulic technology, with the peasant population organized in cooperatives. Although they did not participate directly in the experiments as was originally intended, the participation of an agronomic engineer and hired-hands (from the cooperatives) provided a wealth of ethno-botanic knowledge. Their knowledge of handling native plants also contributed to demonstrate that the raised fields were technically feasible. What was especially noteworthy was their knowledge of plague control and combining native crops in order to set the conditions for two planting seasons in a year (Álvarez 1989).

The results of the agricultural experiments and multidisciplinary research were transferred through an institutional agreement between The Polytechnic University (*Escuela Superior Politénica del Litoral*) ESPOL of Guayaquil, Ecuador, USAID ScD., Washington D.C., and the National Institute for Agriculture and Stock-raising Research (*Instituto Nacional de Investigaciones Agropecuarias*, INIAP)), with the aim of launching a programme aimed at replicating the experiment. We have, however, no evidence this has ever been carried out. The fact that INIAP ignored its agreement to promote this first experience of its kind in Ecuador, and apparently disregarding its importance as a product of multidisciplinary research by a university, evidences the prevailing «institutional discrimination» (Kottak 1994:70) against indigenous cultural products and traditional knowledge.

In general the potential capacity of native technology and knowledge has been underestimated by formal scientific sectors, especially universities and state agencies, making it unlikely for people to appreciate and socially rehabilitate this capacity. We argue here that unless this prejudiced image changes, the balance of power will favour replacing or substituting native technology and knowledge with information produced outside the local culture framework. We propose the alternative of joining both types of knowledge (traditional and modern) with an intercultural approach in order to increase peasant populations' survival and development strategies at a practical level (Claverías, 2002 MS).

The detention pond systems and mestizo populations

In the inventory of Albarradas (detention ponds) systems carried out in the Santa Elena Peninsula (*Península de Santa Elena*, PSE, Ecuador), most systems have been found to be under the local communal or collective property regime[15]. However, some villages with Albarradas systems fall under the national governmental administrative system of cantons and parishes. In general, these latter villages are settlements lying at the periphery of cities, where usage of the Albarradas is marginal (Burmester and Tobar, 2004MS). Although indigenous communes have lower population densities than these settlements, the communes continue to occupy considerable territorial space (Álvarez, 1999).

It is important to note that the mestizo population, despite its lack of self-identification with what is indigenous, know and value the systems much more explicitly than observed among inhabitants of the Lower Guayas River Basin regarding the raised field system.

Cases from El Morro Parrish, Ayalán Hacienda, Paján Canton, Julcuy Parrish or Valle de la Virgen Parrish demonstrate the renovation and updating of these systems, as well as their integration into people's livelihood[16]. In all these cases Albarradas (detention ponds) are working, although their potential is not being fully exploited (Álvarez *et. al.*, 2004).

Since World War II ancient detention ponds have been competing with programmes to build dams or water reservoirs commonly called «*tapes*» [small dams] (Marcos, 2004). Initially, the US Army promoted this type of dam in Ecuador, just as it did in other countries involved in international loans during the so-called Green Revolution (Shiva, 2004:71).[17]

---

15. From 252 recorded Albarradas, 150 (59.5 percent) are under communal regime, while 67 (26.5 percent) belong to private owners, and 28 (11 percent) are open to public use in non-communal areas; for 7 detention ponds (3 percent), there is no reliable data (Marcos, 2004).
16. For more details on each site, see CD annexed to book (J. G. Marcos, Coordinator, 2004).
17. This quote refers to the Maddock Project in Ecuador, a promoter of dams in the Ecuadorian coast during the 1950s (INERHI, 1978).

Sites	El Morro	Ayalán	Paján	Valle de la Virgen	Julcuy
N° of Albarradas	1	10 (3 in public use)	7 in public use	3	6
Main use	Productive-domestic	Productive-domestic	productive	Productive-domestic	Productive-domestic
Maintenance	collective	Collective	individual	collective	collective
Historical reference	Indigenous period	The estate	Modern times	Modern times	Republican period

Throughout the entire region, there are both modern and pre-Colonial or pre-Hispanic *Albarradas* or *Jagüeyes*. An example of modern «Albarradas» is found at Paján Parrish, where state agencies built detention ponds on private lands. Although referred to as *Albarradas* by local farmers, here we propose using the terms «water reservoirs» or «dams» because although they replicate the original model of *Albarradas* or *Jagüeyes* [traditional detention ponds], these have not been built to nurture the subsurface aquifer, preserve the soil or sustain biodiversity (Marcos, 2004). Nor did they chose the site to build these dams by looking for permeable or semi-permeable soils formations that would allow underground water storage and long time conservation. The manifest objectives of these modern reservoirs are to accumulate water on the surface in order to alleviate drought problems, or provide domestic work-sites for women in the region[18].

In most of these sites, some type of maintenance activity on the retaining walls of the modern dams or detention ponds is needed, especially when heavy seasonal rains appear. However, there is no formal or informal organisation, such as an indigenous *Cabildo* [Commune council], which can make these tasks compulsory as a requisite for to access other local resources. Communes follow a criterion of reciprocity; members receive water as part of communal rights and obligations which involve community participation, community work, rights to communal land and water, etc.

We understand that collective usage is inherent and essential to the Albarradas system, and as such has been safeguarded by the prolonged governance of native territory and water management system by the indigenous communities in the region. Therefore, although the concept of private property prevails in non-indigenous areas, the use of Albarradas continues to be unarguably public in the region. This occurs even inside the Ayalán Hacienda, where the «*vivientes*»[19] have access to the water and resources of a number of Albarradas owned by the estate proprietors. During the Republican period, indigenous communities lost control of their resources when cantons and parishes administrators seized these resources, with the exception of water rights, or turned them into private property.

---

18. See detail in Paján Project, CD in Marcos, 2004.
19. «*vivientes*» [live-ins] is the name given to Hacienda hired hands and their families when they live in the property.

In sites like Paján, where there are no communities with a tradition of collective work, the current landowners or users of Albarradas work individually and spontaneously on these dams maintenance. Although many forms of associative experiences exist (i.e. cooperatives, social movements, and clubs), it is in these Albarradas that we have registered an exclusively productive use. At the rest of the sites, domestic (especially hygiene, human consumption, and animal care) is combined with productive use (agriculture, stock-raising, fishing, hunting).

Both in Ayalán and in Valle de la Virgen, albarradas are the only water sources currently available to the area's population; although other eventual sources are privately own wells, and the trucks that sell the liquid to remote villages.[20]

Although inhabitants of Julcuy Parish are aware of their indigenous history, they attribute some of Albarradas to the Republican period in order to support their historic collective rights to those resources. Therefore, with the exception of El Morro Parrish, where the immense albarrada is regarded a legacy from the indigenous era, the remaining sites appear to have no ties with native society.

In interviews, several informants, when referring to the founding history of El Morro by indigenous families in the 18th century informants told us how, by 1764, these families asked the King's permission to settle in the location with 4,000 head of cattle, and there they built the *Albarrada de los Tamarindos*. They cite the surnames Guzmán, Jordán and Cacao as belonging to the indigenous founders of the place (A-003-E-02–1; A-003-OB-01–2). This narration of facts, which has been recorded in the work of Carlos Alberto Flores (1953), was taught to the interviewees at school by teachers who instilled in them a pride in their local history. According to the current inhabitants, the indigenous population disappeared completely after a huge fire devastated at the end of the 19th century. According to locals only the church was spared thanks to the detention water pond (A-003-E-02–1; A-003-E-02–3; A-003-OB-01–2). Educational establishments and oral tradition operate as important sources of indigenous knowledge, and in reproducing resource management and usage norms. Consequently, when traditional rights are subordinated and local culture is underestimated by state officials, identification with these technological systems is lost.

El Morro inhabitants and political leaders recognise the importance of having this Albarrada, and some say they have risked their lives to avoid its destruction during harsh rains and floods. Nonetheless, they are not fully conscious of how it really impinges on domestic and productive reproduction of the village. A test survey carried out in the households around the Albarrada, as well as in close neighbourhoods, allowed us to quantify their habitual use of its water. By quantifying water extracted mainly during the rainy season and the diversified use it is given, we found evidence, beyond what testimonies admit, of the magnitude of this technology's contribution[21]. Free access to Albarrada water is a key means to save money, especially for low-income families. However, instead of stressing its use, people prioritize and grant more social prestige to the water they buy regularly or irregularly from water trucks.

This hierarchical classification of water outlines a scale of social values, not exclusive to this community, in which the water from Albarradas is somewhat stigmatized.

---

20. Water tankers are trucks that habitually sell water for human consumption in most parts of Ecuador.
21. See information in the Albarradas Proyect's database.

Its use is associated with marginalised population sectors living in the countryside or in small villages. This prejudice is exacerbated by institutions that reproduce the dominant culture (school, the media) and even, urban marginal sectors who, though poor, access water from faucets or water-tank trucks. These tankers acquire in the collective imagery a relationship to modernity and prestigious goods that displace local products.

We highlight then, that the rationale that responds to the demands of the capitalist market economy tends to undervalue these traditional systems and replaces such sustainable experience resulting for the accumulated experience and knowledge of native communities throughout centuries. It is obvious, however, that knowledge of the sustainable construction and use of albarradas is broader and more diversified among these mestizo populations than among peasants in cooperatives who own land with raised fields. A fundamental reason for this difference is local indigenous societies' loss of social power over its own resources (Álvarez, 2004MS).

Conclusions

From the anthropological point of view, the Albarradas (traditional detention ponds) and Camellones (raised field systems) are referents that reveal the close relation of native culture and society with nature on the Ecuadorian coast. Nevertheless, this characterization is not recognised by a large portion of the local population that currently benefits from the work and experience accumulated in these traditional (pre-Hispanic) hydraulic systems.

We argue that the social devaluation and loss of knowledge, expressed especially among non-indigenous populations, responds to the establishment and impact of new power relations during the Colonial period. The loss of native communities' power to decide over their territories and resources had a decisive effect on controlling and reproducing these technologies. Although these systems are efficient and suitable for different environmental conditions, they are not adapted to the criteria that guides resource and hand labour exploitation, as established in most of the region. Hence, only territories under indigenous governance maintain and reproduce the technological capital inherited from «the ancient ones». In other regions, this native heritage was substituted by the European experience, and by the interests established by the new relations of power that were consolidated in the *haciendas* and plantations.

At the same time that the subjects who produced pre-Colonial systems were being devalued, their knowledge was also being ignored. Ultimately, this translates into the current population's detachment and loss of knowledge. History that is judged to be uninteresting is neither sought nor reproduced. This also explains the lack of scientific research on native logics and products, and the privilege granted to knowledge that is alien to local culture (i.e., dams).

In Ecuador, disciplines like Archaeology, Geography, and Anthropology have been enquiring into the potential of the indigenous cultural patrimony, and the possibilities of reactivating this patrimony to suit current social needs. Applied scientific research has been limited, however, to quick interventions that unfortunately frequently prefers only tangible results.

This is the case in the Ecuadorian coast, where research on technological systems such as the raised fields and detention ponds are not prioritized by intervention programmes. Since these systems are unknown to development project advocates, they are omitted, or estranged from their original purposes.

In order to formalize the value these systems have for the population, it is crucial to know them better, and then to divulge and promote their use. Scientists need to regard them as an efficient alternative to dominant exogenous models. The proposal of an enlarged reproduction of accumulated native patrimony, recognizing its historical potential[22], needs to be encouraged. In part, this would be achieved by increasing interdisciplinary research, and offering its results to society so people can directly benefit from these studies. It is therefore important to inject an alternative set of dynamics into the exclusively historical knowledge transmitted by the media and most state agents. We therefore conclude that:

Given that government officials and NGO members have no time to recover in-depth data, academics need to hand it to them, through the elaboration of practical and scientific intervention proposals that have been socialized through consultation with communities. Given that the history and sustainability of these systems are transmitted in territories under or influenced by indigenous governance, the empowerment of communities that sustain and reproduce traditional knowledge is vital. Indeed, we recognise the need for adjusting these values and benefits to the population's current development needs.

---

22. For the historical potential of Andean patrimony, see Luis G. Lumberas, personal communication.

Bibliography

Silvia G. Álvarez (1985) Interacción de la Antropología con la Arqueología. Dos ejemplos a la transformación de la realidad en las áreas de programas de desarrollo rural e impacto de grandes obras, *en*: Revista Tecnológica de la Escuela Superior Politécnica del Litoral (ESPOL) Vol.6 (1). pp41-52.

Silvia G. Álvarez (1987) Resiembra de Camellones en la Cuenca del Guayas, en: *Gaceta Arqueológica Andina*, Instituto Andino de Estudios Arqueológicos, INDEA, Año 4 (13): 29-31, Lima.

Silvia G. Álvarez (1989) *Tecnología Prehispánica, Naturaleza y Organización Cooperativa en la Cuenca del Guayas*. Colección Peñón del Río 4, Ed. Centro de Estudios Arqueológicos y Antropológicos, ESPOL, Guayaquil, Ecuador.

Silvia G. Álvarez (1990) Campos de Camellones: la naturaleza modificada a través de la historia, en: *Revista Geográfica,* Instituto Geográfico Militar 28: 153-163 Quito

Silvia G. Álvarez 2004(MS) La renovación de la identidad montubia en el contexto relacional con lo cholo-comunero, ponencia en Simposio Montubio, Globalización, Diversidad Costeña e Identidad Montubia, Archivo Histórico del Guayas, Casa de la Cultura Ecuatoriana, 26-28 de noviembre 2002 (en Prensa).

Álvarez, Silvia G., Martín Bazurco, Mónica Burmester y Claudia González 2004 Componente Sociocultural, Capítulo 5 en: Jorge G. Marcos(Coordinador), Las Albarradas en la Costa del Ecuador: Rescate del conocimiento ancestral del manejo sostenible de la biodiversidad, CEAA-ESPOL, Guayaquil, Ecuador, pp.253-370.

Burmester, Mónica y Oswaldo Tobar 2004(MS) Las albarradas como sistema cultural, la naturaleza como modelo. El ocaso de albarradas antiguas en la provincia del Guayas, Ecuador: Chongón y Muey (manuscrito en poder de los autores)

Claverías, Ricardo 2002 (MS) Conocimientos de los campesinos andinos sobre los predictores climáticos: elementos para su verificación, Centro de Investigación, Educación y Desarrollo (CIED), Lima.

William M. Denevan, Kent Mathewson y Gregory Knapp (eds) 1987 Pre-Hispanic Agricultural Fields in the Andean Region, Part ii, BAR International Series 359 (ii), Proceedings 45 Internatitonal Congress of Americanists, Bogotá, 1985.

Carlos Alberto Flores 1953 [1946] Pueblos y paisajes del Guayas y El Morro y su Comarca, Talleres Gráficos Nacionales, Quito.

González A., Claudia. The future of the albarradas: between local knowledge and «development» policies (This Volume).

INERHI 1978 Presas Península de Santa Elena, Departamento de Relaciones Pública, Quito.

Kottak, Conrad Phillip 1994 Antropología. Una exploración de la diversidad humana con temas de la cultura hispana (*Anthropology. An Exploration of Human Diversity with Topics on Hispanic Culture*), Ed McGraw-Hill, 6th edition

Marcos, Jorge G. 1987 Los campos elevados de la Cuenca del Guayas, Ecuador: El Proyecto Peñón del Río, en: Denevan, Mathewson y Knapp (eds), Pre-Hispanic Agricultural Fields in the Andean Region, Part ii, BAR International Series 359 (ii): 217-224, Proceedings 45 Internatitonal Congress of Americanists, Bogotá, 1985.

Marcos, Jorge G. 1997 El manejo del agua en el variado medioambiente del Área Septentrional Andina, en: M. Guinea; J-F Bouchard; J. G. Marcos (eds), Cultura y Medio Ambiente en el Área Septentrional Andina, 48 Congreso Internacional de Americanistas, Estocolmo-Uppsala julio de 1994, Ed. Abya-Yala, Quito, pp.129–164.

Marcos, Jorge G. 2004 (Coordinador) Las Albarradas en la Costa del Ecuador: Rescate del conocimiento ancestral del manejo sostenible de la biodiversidad, CEAA-ESPOL, Guayaquil, Ecuador.

Marcos, Jorge G. Water Management in Ancient Ecuador (This Volume)

Marcos, Jorge G. & Martín Bazurco 2006 «Albarradas y Camellones en la región costera del Antiguo Ecuador» En. *Agricultura Ancestral. Camellones y Albarradas: Contexto social, usos y retos del pasado y del presente.* Pp.93–110. Ediciones Abya-Yala / IFEA / IRD / Banco Central del Ecuador / INPC / CNRS / Embajada de Francia en Ecuador / Universidad París I

Shiva, Vandana 2004 Las guerras del agua. Contaminación, privatización y negocio, Icaria-Antrazyt Ecología 200, Barcelona.

James J. Parsons & Roy Shlemon 1987 Mapping and dating the prehistoric raised fields of the Guayas basin, Ecuador, en: Denevan, Mathewson y Knapp (eds), Pre-Hispanic Agricultural Fields in the Andean Region, Part ii, BAR International Series 359 (ii), Proceedings 45 Internatitonal Congress of Americanists, Bogotá, 1985.

INTERVIEWS

A-003-E-02–1 RVS (Male, 56 years old) Government Officer and estate proprietor in the Parish, Albarradas Project Database

A-003-E-02–3 CMR (female, 60 years old), MMM (male, 50 years old), RVS (male, 56 years old), NOM (female, 60 years old) El Morro Native and Emigrant Neighbours, Albarradas Project Database

A-003-OB-01–2 Field Observations, Pía Escobar, Albarradas Project Database.

The Future of the Albarradas: Between Local Knowledge and «Development» Policies

Claudia Gonzalez Andricaín

The commoners of the Ecuadorian coast

Many communities descending from the Manteño-Huancavilca culture, on the coastal strip of the Ecuadorian provinces Guayas and Manabí, use and reproduce an ancestral technology for their water provision, the *Albarrada*. Most of these communities have been organized in Communes since the Ecuadorian State approved the Law of Organization and Regime of Communes in 1937 (Álvarez, 2001). This means that settlers have a special legal regime of collective property on territory that includes the *commune*, managed by a communal 'cabildo' (local government) and controlled through the communal assemblies. Although dating in origin too long before the establishment of the Communes, the handling of most of the albarradas in the region is ruled and maintained within the framework of these communal organizations.

The albarradas are earthen structures in a horseshoe form that enable the catchment and storage of rain water, so that the community have a sufficient supply of water for most of the year, if not all year round. On the surface of the collected water community members sow plants that oxygenate it, diminish evaporation, ensure its freshness and help to consolidate a small aquatic ecosystem. They also plant trees in the walls to strengthen them and to provide shade. Another important function of the albarradas is to serve as a support to local biodiversity (Marcos et al. 2004).

In this region, where it rains only once a year and for a short period of time, the rivers are intermittent and quickly dry (Marcos in this volume). This is the crucial reason why an alternative and stable source of water has been very important for these populations. Without the presence of the albarrada technology distributed throughout the territory, the size and the permanence of the present human settlement in the area would have been untenable.

The albarradas may be destroyed in time of abundant rain by the force of the water. Also the *argillaceous* slime that follows the water when it is deposited in the albarrada can block the drainage, or directly diminish its capacity until covering it completely.

For these reasons, only an organized population with experience in creating and maintaining this construction can take proper care of them and ensure that they last.

Recent research has established that the albarradas have been constructed in this region for at least 3500 years (Marcos in this volume), indicating that although not always managed on a communal basis, the populations of the zone have always been organized at least for the management of the water resources. This also holds true for the present. In the cases where the commune is absent, other kinds of local organizations assume the care of the albarradas.

Nowadays, the Communes of the coast constitute a space of political and economic autonomy, and simultaneously a particular socio-cultural space within the coastal region of Ecuador (Alvarez et al, 2002). However, when analyzing the local knowledge concerning the water resource and its implementation, it is necessary to take into account the greater context of regional, national and even international realities.

In this context the most striking feature is the extreme poverty in which these populations live, something that forces them to migrate towards the urban centres in search of work. The numerous programs of development that are being implemented in these communities through governmental and nongovernmental institutions, try to cover the most basic necessities. Another important characteristic is the hard competition that exists between the *communes* and other economic sectors of the region for natural resources, and most fundamentally access to land. This challenge, in addition to serious internal conflicts in the communes, has caused the loss of part of local territory. The condition of poverty in the communes is made worse by the deteriorating environmental conditions encountered in the coastal zone. The climatic change, which causes flash floods and lengthy periods of drought, has made the economy of this population more fragile.

All these factors create a hostile environment for the survival of the communes. The capacities for social, material and symbolic reproduction of these communities have been debilitated. This worsening situation of local people affects their possibilities of valuation and of putting into practice their local knowledge, experience and management of the natural resources, including the albarradas.

Systems of water supplying

The presence of the albarradas in the region over many centuries, gives us an idea of how important they are for the local population in the specific environmental surroundings in which they live. Moreover, they indicate the importance of traditional knowledge concerning these ancestral structures- knowledge that although not static and unchanging has persisted in these communities for many generations, in spite of the dramatic rupture of the Spanish colonization.

In order to achieve a deep understanding about this technology, it's important to acknowledge that albarradas are complex structures with social, environmental and physical dimensions. Amongst other things we can point out the following components:
- accumulated knowledge that allows the handling of the environment;
- organized collective ability to work;
- norms, values and conducts that orient management of the natural resources;

- physical structure of the albarrada;
- associated structures, wells of water inside and outside the albarrada, wharves, laundries (Marcos et al. 2004).

Analysis of the albarrada *per se* allows us to see how eco-cultural strategies and organization strategies for its proper operation are combined. A focused study of the albarrada system moreover helps us to see how it is managed in a collective and harmonious way, and with respect to factors like aquatic and terrestrial plants, animal species, run-offs of rain, types of ground, gradient of lands, existence of the aquifers and climatic events. This is all part of the local knowledge that local people possess and that has been transmitted orally and through practice in communal activities.

The elements mentioned so far articulate and ensure that the albarrada work as a system. Nevertheless, through fieldwork we realized that the albarradas were not always used as isolated units. The communities frequently articulated specific uses of albarradas based on characteristics like size, location and with respect to the centre of population, access of cattle and quality of water. Hence they tend to use various types of albarradas for different purposes, confirming what we conceive of as «systems of albarradas» (Álvarez et al, 2004).

In some communities there are no more water sources than the albarradas and some wells. But, in the majority of the communities the systems of albarradas are integrated into larger water supply systems, along with 'modern' technologies of water provision such as cisterns that loads water, big containers in the populated centres, CEDEGÉ[23] channel and piped water networks.

In this sense we can say that the set of functions that albarradas have has not been totally displaced by the new technologies; instead they have changed and been fitted into other systems. But this incorporation has not materialized as a combination of diverse, «equal», and complementary knowledge. We have observed that new patterns (arbitrary and external) of valuing the qualities of water, underestimate the importance of the albarradas (Jacobsen in this volume). Many professionals and technicians of the development institutions that work in the region, and also local people that live in the cities consider this technology to be backward. In addition, some water merchants discredit the traditional water sources in order to booster their own business in the communities. In our research in the area we have not come across any comparative and reliable study concerning the quality of water from different sources. Despite the fact that no such comparative study of water quality exists, it has been assumed, a priori, that modern technology is a quality assurance, and that the water of the albarradas is unsanitary.

What our research does demonstrate is that, contrary to what has been expected, the introduction of new water technology in the communities has not improved the access to the water of the general population. Some evident problems may be pointed out:
- Access to the water of the car tanks or the piped water depends on the buying capacity of each family, a reason why the poorest families of the communities that neglected their albarradas, have problems to replace their necessities and in some cases they are becoming indebted. Moreover, due to the problem of cost, families

---

23. Channel constructed since Daule River to Santa Elena Peninsula.

located on a hill. This elevated water tank was also connected to five public water taps placed at strategic locations around the settlement.

As in other communities local people prefer to have the taps in their own homes, so they constructed connecting hoses in order to direct the water from the public taps into their homes. When, on his next visit, the foreign technician saw the hoses going into the houses he got very angry, and pull them out. His argument was that the public taps were necessary to create a good sense of community in the commune. The inhabitants complained about this means, insisting that a good neighbourhood does not depend on public taps. The insistence on public taps forces them to have to carry the water to their houses. In the end a situation aroused where the commune put someone in charge of watching when the technician approached and to be able run and hide hoses before his arrival. In other words, these people are forced to act secretly because a NGO technician did not want to reflect on the clash of communitarian ideals, or the financial aims of the project.

This is a typical example of an imposition of external ideas on a community, as well as of ignorance of the traditional water management of the communes of the Coast. In these communities, collective traditional practices during the workings of construction and maintenance of the communitarian water structures are carried out, although access to water in itself is realized by individuals and families. To put hoses into the houses did not change the communitarian practices of Manantial de Guangala.

Construction of «Tapes» versus construction of Albarradas

The historical success of the albarradas systems have attracted the attention of different institutions related to the management of hydrological resources. As a strategy to solve the scarcity of water, some institutions tried to reproduce this traditional technology. This strategy, carried out in a context of ignorance about local knowledge and structural features of the albarrada, produced a new hydrological structure: the so-called *tapes*.

The fundamental difference between a *tape* and an albarrada, is that albarrada only use weak run-offs created by the rainfall in order to catch water. In the case of the tapes, a wall is constructed blocking a river, a brook, or a strong run off, with the purpose of guaranteeing sufficient water collection during merely one rainy season. Sometimes Albarradas need more than one rainy season to fill up. The disadvantage of constructing structures that collect water from a weak run off is that less water is cached in one rain season than in a tape. However, the advantage is that there is less chance that the wall will break and for the structure to be destroyed in periods of flood.

In terms of effectiveness, albarradas have been shown to be more durable and reliable than tapes. Actually, about 60% of the tapes broke in one winter season with heavy rainfall (Marcos *et al.* 2004). This is a very important fact if monetary investments, community work and the expectations that are put into these types of projects. The tapes are yet another example of a failed investment which the technicians of the development institutions impose on a community, in form of a type of 'external' construction to replace a traditional technology. They believed that they were improving traditional technology, but without knowing sufficiently the physico-ecological characteristics of the old structures.

The albarrada of Sacachún

One of the most important development institutions, with strong ties to the major indigenous organization in Ecuador, CONAIE[26], decided to carry out a project in the Sacachún Commune. That project aimes to construct an albarrada whose water would irrigate a collective orchard. The technicians describe the project as geared toward agricultural production. Their proposal was presented to the community and in the communal Assembly several community members pointed out that the albarradas were not designed for irrigation. In their opinion the construction of a well connected to an elevated tank would be more appropriate. In other words, the communal priorities were, in a first place, a water system that allows families to have water directly accessible in their houses, and in second place, an albarrada for domestic tasks, near the centre of Sacachún.

Whilst the land in the communes is communal, their work and use is familiar. The creation of a public orchard breaks this conception and imposes an investment of time and extra effort that the Sacachún community are not used to assume. In any case, in the commune (at internal level) the project was understood as an unwanted imposition. Additionally, commoners considered that the amount of water in an albarrada would be insufficient for agricultural production for more than 30 families. Commoners wanted an albarrada, or an elevated tank near the community, with the purpose of supplying of water for the domestic tasks and the daily consumption. Such local priorities should have been considered by the development institution carry out evaluations during its field visits: where it is desired to construct the albarrada, what for, the accessibility to people, the accessibility to the cattle, how many families would benefit, what alternative uses can be considered so that the productivity of the community is really enhanced, etc.

Unfortunately, the technicians did not pay attention to this request. The technicians of this development institution were only willing to finance a project aimed at economic production, and they moreover refused to accept a proposal for a productive project aimed at supporting family based production. Once more an idyllic representation of a commune does not match reality, and it is imposed on the community through a development project, and the management strategies of the albarradas are ignored.

Final reflections

The Albarradas are complex structures that have enabled these populations for many centuries to obtain and use water in a sustainable and equitable way. Their construction and operation are based, on the one hand, in the articulated application of the local knowledge on diverse elements of the environment, and on the other hand, in the native forms of organization and management of the resource. This technology is an

---

26. Confederation of Indigenous Nationalities of Ecuador.

element of the modern local knowledge but a background in the traditional echo-cultural patrimony of the communes of coastal Ecuador.

In spite of the existence of this rich and diverse echo-cultural patrimony in this region of Ecuador, a symmetrical intercultural relationship that allows to the complementation and interchange of diverse knowledge does not exist. The results of sociocultural investigation made by the Albarradas project demonstrate a scenario in which the autochthonous knowledge of the communes is rejected in spite of its historical effectiveness. Such rejection has had the consequence of eroding the local strategies and technologies of the communes. In a context of social inequality the quality of life has also been diminished, because local people do not have access to 'modern' technologies.

Although is not intentional, the development institutions contribute to a breakdown in the local pattern of management of water resources. The development model that technicians apply has not been able to surpass cultural asymmetry existing in the entire region, and their 'participative' methodology although based on a vindication and respect towards the communes has proved to be more rhetoric than reality. Participation and intercultural relationship should be a constant and natural practice and not a formal requirement.

This asymmetric context allows for external to impose a foreign technology, as well as a non local rationality of the water consumption based on a wrong stereotype of the way of communal life. The case of Sacachún, an external conception of a communal agricultural production (in shape of a collective orchard) has been imposed, combined with another external conception of the albarrada, as a water source for agriculture.

The other two cases demonstrate how the attempts to reproduce a technology without knowing it thoroughly, or to impose an external technology that supposedly acts as the same («tape»), results not only in the loss of money, but as in the case of San Marcos, can put in risk the weak communal infrastructure or even the very lives of local people. The tapes and the dam of San Marcos constitute clear examples of a process of technological imposition and fragmentation of local knowledge.

I have shown only four cases, but most of the projects have been applied through by-passing the local mechanisms of control and management and the aspirations of the commoners themselves (González, 2002). This new reality put in serious danger the continuity of communal management of the water through the albarradas, and the people's own conception of what an albarrada is and what it serves for. It is evident in the cases in which the albarradas are taken into account -in most of the projects the technology are invisible and under valuated- but imposing «new» priorities of the communes.

Such results compel us to see the necessity of knowing and valuing traditional technologies and the accumulated local knowledge of the communes of the Ecuadorian coast. This recognition is especially imperative for the development institutions, because of their impact on local realities. Local patterns of water management have offered and offer real possibilities for an ecologic and equitable access, which can contribute very well to the sustainable development of the Communes. It is impossible to achieve a sustainable communal development through the alienation of its history, its patrimony and the knowledge accumulated for hundreds of years.

Bibliography

Álvarez, Silvia. 2001. *De Huancavilcas a Comuneros. Relaciones interétnicas en la Península de Santa Elena, Ecuador.* Quito: Abya Yala, 2nd edition.

Álvarez S, Bazurco M, Burmester M, Escobar P, Gonzáles C, Arias O. 2002. Capital Social comunal en la costa del Ecuador: nuevos retos y desafíos en la globalización. In Piqué R, Ventura M. (eds.): *América Latina Historia y Sociedad: Una visión interdisciplinaria. Cinco años de 'Aula Oberta' en la UAB.* Barcelona, Catalunya, España. Institut Català de Cooperació Iber.americana, 135–147.

Álvarez S, Bazurco M, Burmester M, Gonzáles C. 2004. Organización social, cultura y gestión de los Sistemas de Albarradas en la Península de Santa Elena. Chap.5 In Marcos, Jorge G. (ed.): *Las Albarradas en la Costa del Ecuador: Rescate del conocimiento ancestral del manejo de la biodiversidad.* Guayaquil, Ecuador: CEAA/ESPOL, pp. 253–370.

Becerra, Carlos et al. 2001. *Las ONGs y el modelo neoliberal. Caso Guayas.* Quito, Ecuador: Abya Yala and Ecuadorian Institute for Social Development.

Bretón, Víctor. 2001. *Cooperación al desarrollo y demandas étnicas en los Andes ecuatorianos.* Quito, Ecuador: FLACSO.

Escobar, Arturo. 1996. *La invención del tercer mundo, construcción y deconstrucción del desarrollo.* Santa Fé de Bogotá, Colombia: Norma.

FISE (Social Investment fund of Emergency). 2004. *Guides of the Communitarian Diagnosis.* Presidency of the republic, Ecuador.

González A., Claudia. 2003. *Identidades étnicas en acción. La organización comunal de la Península de Santa Elena ante la Cooperación al Desarrollo.* Master Thesis. Universidad Autónoma de Barcelona, Department of Social Anthropology and Prehistoria, Division of Social Anthropology. Bellaterra.

Marcos, Jorge G. (ed.) 2004. *Las Albarradas en la Costa del Ecuador: Rescate del conocimiento ancestral del manejo de la biodiversidad.* Guayaquil, Ecuador: CEAA/ESPOL.

Two Stories about Development on the Peninsula Santa Elena, Ecuador[27]

Frode F. Jacobsen

Introduction

When thought about, a story may be like wandering in a mythical landscape, where the storyteller is inviting the listener on a journey moving past places that carry a specific significance for the narrator. Naturally not every single detail in that landscape is relevant to a given narrative; narration involves both the skill of remembering and of forgetting. The process of remembering past experiences imbues the mythical landscape with meaning (Johansen 1988). Indeed, wandering in a mythical landscape sometimes accompanies a real journey in which a village here or a tree or a stone there invokes memories of past experiences. A narrative may therefore be viewed as a means of presenting the past in a way that imbues the present with meaning and creates certain expectations about the future, shaping an experience of individual continuity (selfsameness) and the continuity of ones culture and society (Bruner 1990; Friedman 1994; Labov 1982).

I want to share with the reader two stories that both relate to a concrete geographical area, the semi-arid area of the Peninsula Santa Elena in coastal Ecuador, and the *comuneros*, the peasant majority of the population inhabiting this areas. Since three years ago I have had the privilege to get to know the area, its inhabitants and their ingenious local forms of water harvesting systems through the multi-disciplinary Albarrada research team in Ecuador, represented by three of the authors in this volume, Jorge Marcos, Silvia Alvarez and Claudia Gonzalez Andricain.

The stories to be presented here represent a peculiar kind of narrative in the respect that the narrator is not directly a part of what is told. The stories are stories about others, about people with whom the narrators contrast, rather than identify, themselves.

---

27. Thanks to Claudia Gonzalez and Martín Bazurco, PhD students at La Universidad Autónoma de Barcelona, Spain, dr. John McNeish, University of Bergen, Norway, and prof. Jorge Marcos, Escuela Superior Politécnica del Litoral (ESPOL), Guayaquil, Ecuador, for valuable comments upon earlier drafts of this chapter.

Actually I aim to present two examples of «expert stories». They are expert stories in the sense that they are stories from people generally held to be experts on community development at an Ecuadorian university.

The stories relate to the social and economic development on the Peninsula Santa Elena, Ecuador and to a period in which the British company *The Ancon Oil Company of Ecuador Limited* had started to exploit oil resources in the area called La Punta de Santa Elena, on the tip of the peninsula in 1911 (for details, see Estrada 2001). The stories represent two very different kinds of expert stories. The stories I heard from academics during the Fall 2003, who were both affiliated with an Ecuadorian university and simultaneously doing consultancies for various NGOs[28] and GOs[29], could be grouped into two main versions on development on Peninsula Santa Elena since 1911. As soon will become evident to the reader, my position is far from an objective and uninvolved observer being guilty as I am of having sparked through conversations both types of stories. Still I hope that I manage to do at least some justice to both versions and to demonstrate how particular views of social and economic sustainability and development may have implications for how the present situation of the peasant population of the peninsula is portrayed, and how a particular understanding of the present has implications for the depiction of a historical past and a future scenario.

The first story

The first time I heard the first story, was during a trip in a car belonging to the university, together with one of the top officials of the university named 'Pedro', who has been a leader of a large scale research and development project on the Peninsula Santa Elena run jointly by his university and state agencies. We were travelling through a semi-arid landscape typical of the peninsula, with a scarcity of trees caused by local people cutting trees for charcoal production, according to the official. We went past a place named after a local type of tree, and he exclaimed, «Isn't that ironic? There is no single example of this tree left any more. People have cut them all in order to produce charcoal. Still the place carries its name…». He went on to explain how a lot of negative things have happened on the peninsula since 1911, when the British oil company arrived:

«In 1911 the British came and began to exploit the oil resources in Ancón. They found a lot of oil and of good quality, the best quality in the whole of Ecuador. […] Many jobs were created and people came from all over the peninsula to work. For two or three generations much people were employed there. They forgot all their previous knowledge and skills, both agriculture and cattle breeding. They also became incapable of taking care of the vegetation. They began to make charcoal, and now there are almost no trees left on the peninsula. When the British withdrew in 1976 the local people were not able to cater for their own subsistence, because they didn't possess the agricultural skills of their forefathers any longer. We[30] *have initiated several projects where we teach local people agriculture, and to combine agriculture with cattle*

---

28. Non-government organisations
29. Government organisations

breeding and with planting of new trees. We also aim at achieving more biodiversity. However, we have to teach the local people everything from scratch.»

Our trip went on, lasting the whole day. We made several stops, talking to local people and representatives of university and development projects. At one point we made a stop to talk to a man from South Manabi, an area bordering the peninsula in the north, and an area where people share many cultural and social traits with the population of the peninsula (Marcos *et al.* 2004). According to Pedro, the man was one of the most successful examples of local peasants who have adopted «improved» agricultural techniques for irrigation, ploughing and crop selection. He added: «He is not really from the area; he just married a local girl here. He is willing to learn and to change, and he demonstrates a lot of initiative, unlike other local people here».

After chatting with the man, we walked for a while on foot, passing by animals grassing on the meagre pasture of the area, and Pedro commented: «Do you observe how thin and unhealthy the animals look? People here don't really care for their animals. They just let them roam around freely, without providing them with any other food than the grass and bushes that the animals can find by themselves». I asked him how things were in former times, and he told me that «Their forefathers knew how to take good care of the animals, but nowadays this knowledge is all lost. Still people keep a lot of animals, and they all look like this, as you can see». He also showed me some trees planted as part of a joint project of the university and an NGO, stating that «people need a change in their mentality. We steadily have to return to look after the trees, they don't seem to care for them themselves».

At another point we went through a village were people were out in the streets making preparations for a big religious celebration, starting the next day. Pedro stated that, «Soon people here will get very drunk. Then they start to remember all their past grievances, and after a while they get into quarrels and fights. They celebrate a lot; sometimes one celebration immediately follows the other. They are really good for nothing.»

Before going into more details about Pedro's story and his various comments about the local population, let us have a closer look at some of the characteristics of the local people and their adaptation to the natural conditions of the peninsula.

Ethnicity, local knowledge and water management in Peninsula Santa Elena

The Peninsula of Santa Elena is, from a natural resource perspective, a rather marginal area. The peninsula is a semi-desert area with a lack of easily accessible ground water,[31] and where the soil is mostly thin and salty. The fluctuation of the tropical rainstorm of El Niño largely determines the climate through its creation of a deluge of rain in years where it is active, and severe drought when it is not. An ingenious ancient local water harvesting system, with a special type of detention ponds called *albarradas,* has up to

---

30. 'We' refers both to his university and a state development organization working together with the university.
31. Except from an area around the Rio Verde, situated in the south-western part of the peninsula. Otherwise the ground water exists 30–100 m below the ground (Marcos, personal communication).

this day been a traditional way of catching the superficial runoff before it reaches the seashore.

The peninsula is mainly inhabited by descendents of Indian groups that have resided in the area for probably more than 6000 years (Álvarez 2002). This area was never under direct control of the Inca; nor was it very interesting for the Spanish colonialists, who found few valuable resources in the area to exploit, or indeed for NGOs, catholic and protestant missionaries. In opposition to the language situation in the Andes Mountains, the peninsula population became Spanish speaking around 200 years ago. This has helped them in obtaining formal common property rights for their ancestral land and to a much higher degree than Indian populations in the Andes.

There are no distinct ethnic markers today that set the largely peasant population of the peninsula apart from other peasants along the coast of Ecuador. Nevertheless they tend to view themselves as different from other mestizos, without specifying what precisely the difference is. Pedro and a couple of others from his university that I spoke to described them as peasants, but as a less developed kind of peasants. One of them even added that «the Indians in the mountains are more progressive than the people here [on the peninsula]. People here are of a rather useless kind». They are usually not viewed by outsiders as native, and few people on the peninsula explicitly portray themselves as natives (Bazurco 2006), although there is a growing pressure from organizations like CONAIE[32] for local populations in Ecuador to define themselves as native (Bazurco 2006; Selverston 1994). CONAIE is the largest Ecuadorian political organization for indigenous groups and has been vital in propagating the rights of indigenous groups in Ecuador. However, since most people of the Peninsula Santa Elena do not regard themselves as indigenous, they scarcely benefit from the political achievements of the CONAIE.

This said. two 'ethnic' organizations claiming to represent the communities of Santa Elena have lately been established, the Federación de Comunas del Guayas (FCG), and the Movimiento Indígina de los Pueblos Mata, Huancavilca Y Puná (MIPMAWPU). MIPMAWPU have so far not achieved any substantial support from the local population, while FCG is an older and more established organization of the Peninsula Santa Elena, experiencing more support from the local population. Nevertheless, the FCG has little political influence in the wider society of Ecuador since it is not regarded as a proper indigenous organization by the other indigenous organizations or by society at large.[33]

Collective ownership of land is quite widespread on the peninsula, as is the common management of water resources. The *albarrada* is a device for the collective management of water harvesting that is spread out throughout much of the peninsula. At first glance they look like natural pools of water, but on closer inspection turn out to be man-made detention ponds designed to capture runoff from rains and requiring complex local knowledge for construction, maintenance and use. Albarradas are really «artificial wetlands» contributing to sustainable use of natural resources (see Marcos, this volume). They vary both in size and form; some of them merely a few hundred square meters, while others are larger structures of several thousand square meters, some are

---

32. Confederación de Nacionalidades de Indígenas del Ecuador
33. Martín Bazurco, contributing to this book, oral communication.

circular, others horseshoe shaped and yet others are elongated structures with a «tail» (Marcos et al. 2004). These structures are capable of supplying the communities with water most of the year, and frequently, all the year round (Gonzalez Andricaín, this volume).

In contrast to efforts by national and international NGOs at constructing water harvesting systems on the peninsula, where the constructions frequently fail and are easily destroyed by the heavy el Niño rainstorm, the traditional earthen albarrada structures are well adapted to the natural environment and to local climatic conditions. In addition, albarradas serve as «reservoirs» of a great biodiversity, where around 180 plants previously thought to be endemic to the Galapagos a couple of years ago have been documented to exist in and around the albarradas. The oldest ones date back at least 3800 years, and are associated with the Late Valdivia occupation c. 2000–1800 BC (Marcos et al. 2004; see also Marcos this volume).

A different story

The fact that local knowledge concerning the maintenance and use of albarradas is still present and actively put to use in local communities all over the peninsula (ibid.), indicates that the story claiming the near total loss of local knowledge among the general population is too simple. Having presented the first type of story to another group of researchers at the same local university, I was given in return a very different story about what happened on the peninsula since 1911. One of the group, 'Carlos', commented that «This story is a typical NGO story that you will hear from many people here. In reality, this is the dominating account that you will encounter here». One of Carlos' colleagues went on to provide another very different story:

> «In reality this is what happened: In 1911 the British arrived and acquired an exclusive right to exploit coastal oil resources. Many workers were attracted to their project and got employment. The workers asked the British for gas for cooking, but the British wanted to keep the resources for themselves and didn't want to share with the local population. In order to meet their demand for fuel the British asked for help from Colombia. People on the peninsula had never ever earlier burnt charcoal. For this reason expertise in charcoal production was imported from Colombia, in order to teach the trade to locals. As a result of this policy deforestation became an increasing problem, a process that still goes on in areas where there are a few trees left. People haven't forgotten how to cultivate and raise livestock. People who moved to Ancon always kept in contact with rural areas and cultivation activities there, and after each rainy season they went back to their original land to cultivate. The same practice continues today. Even people in Guayaquil have not severed their links to the rural areas and agricultural activities there. The peninsula is characterized by scarcity in natural resources and cultivation is for this reason very demanding. It is hence important for us to first learn what they know, and start our relief work from there.»

Some days later I was introduced to 'Ana', a colleague of Pedro and Carlos, who clearly subscribed to the first kind of expert story. She also told a related story to me and to several students gathered to obtain information about a new relief project initiated by the university and a foreign NGO. Her story is based on her own experiences from dealing with the population of an urbanity near Ancón and focuses on a problem they had with an albarrada in the middle of their settlement.

Ana tells us:

«Local people must be taught about the biodiversity of their area, both in the littoral zone and connected with their albarradas. We have initiated various projects where their children can learn about this. The local people no longer appreciate their traditional technology. We have to teach them, and provide them with the knowledge that their forefathers used to have and which they have since long forgotten. In [mentioning the name of the village] people don't want their albarrada any longer. They have asked us to remove it. They tell us that the albarrada frequently floods and that its walls crack causing the destruction of nearby houses. People have built too high walls and moved their houses too close to the albarrada. We cannot let people destroy their albarrada. This would be just like allowing people to commit suicide. We cannot defend ethically that people destroy this valuable technology which their forefathers have developed for at least the last 4000 years.»

This particular story was very much at odds with stories that I had heard earlier about the so-called conservativism of the local people i.e. their resistance to new technology and fierce defence of traditional solutions and technology. I presented the story to Carlos and a couple of other researchers who had produced the second type of story. Again I got a very different story:

«You know, «bad water» has for many locals become equivalent to «poor people's water». Water from the albarradas has come to symbolize underdevelopment both for many NGO officials and for representatives of the local population, who has come to internalize the attitude of the NGO officials. When some NGO people working there proposed to purify water by adding chlorine to it, local people took it seriously and added chlorine to the albarrada water. I don't know if any of the NGO officials actually told them to add chlorine into the albarrada itself, maybe they just told people how to purify water in general by using chlorine. Anyhow, local people had internalized the view that albarrada water is not good water and hence added a large amount of chlorine in it. As a result, all the living organisms in the water died and the whole structure became like a graveyard. The smell of stinking fish and rotting plants was rather unpleasant for people living nearby, and they asked the NGO people to help get rid of the whole albarrada.»

I further asked the researchers about the problem of broken walls, and 'Maria', a close colleague of Carlos, told me that:

«Until recently, people in the community used to build walls the old way, by taking sediment from the bottom of the albarrada and added it to the walls [Earlier I had been told that such a method of slowly increasing the size of the walls by adding successive layers of sediments from the bottom of the albarrada made them much more

stable]. Nowadays NGOs use caterpillars to dig up soil from the bottom to increase the size of the walls. These walls will not resist large flows of water, something that causes damages to the nearby houses. Even worse, Pedro [the already introduced university official] had built a new wall where water originally used to run freely into the albarrada from the slopes, and inserted pipes in the new wall with too small a dimension to allow for sufficient passage of the El Niño water. This new wall will break down for sure, causing great damage».

All university representatives involved in that community to some extent made the same observation, that the present albarrada does not function properly and that the local people want it removed. However, their agreement stopped there. There was an obvious divide within the research community with basically two main orientations towards the present situation, past history and future of the local population of the Peninsula Santa Elena. Representatives of both main positions seemingly get their views confirmed by observing present failures of albarrada development, such as those described above.

Expert camps and contested representations of local communities

Experts adhering to the first type of story seemed to view cultural, social and economic development in terms of increased technological complexity and increased involvement in market economy. To my experience, engineers of various kinds tend to dominate among these experts both in terms of political influence and in share numbers, although also some people from within the fields of pedagogy and social science support their main views on development and the *comuneros*. People belonging to the «engineer camp», all having a relatively short history of involvement with the local communities (three years at most), tend to view the past of the local population on the peninsula as a time when people knew how to keep cattle, harvest water and take care of their biodiversity. Their present is characterized by social and cultural decline and by the degradation of natural resources, where the locals themselves are to blame for this unfortunate situation. The humble living conditions and the subordinate position that characterize most of the present population may give strength to such prejudice (see Alvarez, this volume). A possible future scenario could either be one of further disintegration and decline or a situation where external experts succeed in helping them on the right track, in terms of recapturing «lost» knowledge and of integrating them into the state and wider systems of market economy.

While experts of the engineer camp, who stick to the first type of story, tend to stress the social and cultural discontinuity of the population, experts supporting the second type of story, with backgrounds in different disciplines such as archaeology, anthropology and biology and a relatively long record of involvement with the local communities (up to 23 years), maintain that local people still possess valuable local knowledge that has enabled them to adapt in a sustainable way to their natural environment. Their view of the present is characterized by an unequal competition between locally developed ways of utilizing natural resources and external and frequently disruptive influences from state organizations and NGOs. A rather bleak future for the local is frequently portrayed, where external initiatives continue to undermine local ways of coping with a challenging natural environment. However, some hope is now and then expressed that at least a substantial part of the population will still be able to cling to their collective land and to reproduce and develop their traditional knowledge and skills.

While the experts of the engineer camp give a rather gloomy picture of the present social and cultural state of affairs among the local communities they spoke highly about their cultural past. For example Ana, a social scientist, depicts the albarradas as «a valuable technology which their forefathers have developed for at least the last 4000 years». Such a split position has also been described by the educational researcher Aurolyn Luykx for proponents of present language ideologies in Bolivia and several countries in the Andean region. While the antique grammatical language forms in native languages are looked upon as genuine and as part of a great and heroic Indian past, present spoken Indian languages are viewed as «corrupted» by external influences and present social and cultural decadence and disruption (Luykx 2003). While present native people are «good for nothing», their forefathers were heroic and skilful.

Even some romantization of their present situation was made by some of the representatives of the engineer camp, who praised local people for sharing everything, for having no individual property and collective work in all productive tasks. The present and historical existence of individual plots for horticulture and the fact that water collection was done independently by individual households were local realities that were not included in this romantic picture.

A peculiar blend of romanticism and stigmatization seemed to prevail among these academics. Besides portraying comuneros as collectively oriented, they were also described as backward people not sufficiently integrated into the modern economy, and, on the other side, as quarrelsome people not capable of cooperating with their neighbours. Such a double attitude of romanticism and stigmatization is curiously reminiscent of the descriptions given by British colonial officers in African countries (Comaroff & Comaroff 1992:247):

«There was no private property, no commerce, no sign of «healthy, individualistic competition» or the maximization of time and effort that the Christians saw as righteous industry (Mackenzie quoted in Dachs 1972:652). As Reverend Willoughby (n.d.) put it, «The African lives a simple socialistic life, subordinating his individuality to the necessities of the tribe» ».

A vision of a healthy economic future for the local peninsula population in the engineer camp peculiarly enough does *not* include a further development of their livestock production, but rather development of irrigated agricultural schemes focusing geared toward cash crops. Their expressed hope of a future scenario was of intensified agricultural production where people stay put in fixed localities and work hard on their land instead of «roaming around» with their animals. Again this is an image that closely mirrors the British colonial dream for Africa, in the words of Comaroff & Comaroff (1992:246):

«In the seventeenth century, Spenser had advocated a settled agrarian existence as the solution to the problem of the «wild Irish», whose barbarous and warlike state he ascribed to their semi-nomadic, pastoral pursuits (Muldoon 1975:275). Similar notions were carried to the new world and Africa, for they corresponded with what Europeans had come to regard as the natural evolution of their own superior world. Agriculture made men peaceful, law-abiding, and governable».

An engineer-driven vision of a more «developed» agriculture on the Peninsula Santa Elena has involved efforts at using water from the albarradas for irrigation, a use of the albarradas that is not known to the comuneros. In most cases the local population has resisted such efforts, and there has been no sign of success in the few cases where the development of albarradas for irrigation has been carried out. This resistance is frequently mentioned by the researchers in the engineer camp as evidence of the conservative attitude of the locals. They tended to interpret the lack of enthusiasm among the comuneros to follow up on tree-planting projects as a sign of local people's resistance toward development. While these researchers regarded this as proof of a need for a change in people's mentality, the researchers supporting the second and alternative story questioned the legitimacy of those projects:

«They don't ask the local people what they want. When we ask people about the tree-planting, they tell us that «we don't want trees, we want a forest!» They do not want a collection of a single species of tree. Moreover, people don't believe in the way that the developers go about planting, starting high up in a slope where the earth is very dry and plant downwards toward the settlements. For them, starting to plant near the albarradas makes more sense».

Conclusion

Telling a story is like presenting a collection of family pictures, where both the selection and order of the pictures fits into a project where the narrator establishes meaning by creating a sense of historical continuity, making daily experiences into a coherent narrative (Bruner 1990). The perception of the present state of affairs influences in this manner which «pictures» to forget and which ones to choose when creating a story, or vice versa, the pictures are selected that make the present most meaningful to the narrator. Experts of the engineer camp excluded the element of British efforts at educating people in burning of charcoal, while including the fact about labour migration to Ancon. While experts from the alternative camp did not speak explicitly about the process of local labour migration, they stressed in particular the unwillingness of the British to share the petroleum resources with the locals and their import of Colombian workers to teach the locals charcoal production. When relating to the story of the abandoned albarrada, they focused on the Chlorine catastrophe, an element not included in the story of academics from the engineer camp.

Clearly, the engineer-dominated perspective on cultural and social resources of the locals differs substantially from the perspective of the alternative camp. The differences in perspective may account for which details in the past history of the comuneros choose to include and leave out. It is too simple, however, merely to state the differences and how the various actors present the past of the locals result from a process of selectively choosing among relevant historical facts. The past does not present itself to anyone in an objective manner. Indeed, it is not only the selection and combination process that is a creative process, but also the establishment of the facts themselves. In other words, picking relevant pictures is not only a process of choice between alternatives, but also a cultural process of *establishing* the pictures to present.

This latter point is aptly illustrated by the differences in presentation of the same basic facts related to the establishment of the British petroleum industry in Ancón and increased production of charcoal by the local population propelled by that incidence. In both main types of stories it is made clear that people increasingly burned charcoal for household fuel. In the type of story told by people from the engineer camp, these facts are described as resulting from a social and cultural discontinuity caused by a change in work adaptation after the introduction of the British industry. The perceived discontinuity and the resulting lack of knowledge in the present population regarding management of natural resources legitimizes the involvement by present developers where the aim is to teach the locals both how to regain the knowledge of their forefathers and require new knowledge and a set of new practices in accord with modern market economy development.

In the alternative set of stories, however, the knowledge that the local population possess is more important than teaching them how to change and encourage a «mentality shift» in them. From that point of view the disruptive interrelationships between the locals and external agents like the British has been the main reason behind the increased burning of charcoal. Representatives from both camps present the past of local people in a manner that appears meaningful in the context of their view of the present situation of the locals. Their narrative projects both create certain expectations (and fears) about the future and legitimize different courses of action.

The experts from the engineer camp envision a future of increased agricultural production and market integration for the local population, and view themselves as legitimate educators and proponents of modern development. The experts from the alternative camp seem in general less optimistic about the future of the comuneros, pointing to the vision of the engineer camp as posing a real threat toward the sustainability of the local communities, and stressing the dominance of the engineer camp both in terms of number of academics and in terms of national and international funding for their projects. They hope for a future of increased control by the local population over their own natural, social and cultural resources. In their view the locals already possess valuable knowledge enabling them to cope with the rather rough natural environment of the peninsula and a long history of relating to external demands in a flexible manner, through long-distance trade and other ways of cooperation. Instances of cutting of live trees and bushes are not explained by the people from the alternative camp as evidence of lack of relevant knowledge, but rather as evidence of decreasing living conditions sometimes forcing local people to act in favour of short term survival rather than long term sustainability, as exemplified by one of them by citing a local woman: «It is my tree or my son».

The different stories presented by the two camps are of course not only two alternative stories having an equally strong influence on how the comuneros are presented to the wider society, both nationally and internationally. In terms of political influence and economic funds the «engineer camp» has the upper hand in the struggle to present the «true» story of the peninsula population, even though their exposure to the local communities has been of a relatively short duration. It may be fair to state that the engineer camp, stressing the lack of cultural and organizational continuity on the peninsula, themselves represent a lack of continuous involvement in the communities both in terms of the overall time span of their involvement and in terms of the mostly short duration of their field visits. There is no reason to believe that they are the only actors on the NGO scene on the peninsula to held prejudices about the comuneros. However, their prejudices definitely have a larger impact on the lives of the local population than the prejudices of other outsiders involving themselves with the locals. The conceptions the «engineer» camp has of the peninsula population do not only spread more forcefully in the outside world, but also tend to materialize both rapidly and dramatically through actions that have huge consequences for the natural environment of the peninsula and the adaptation of the local population to their natural environment.

Bibiliography

Álvarez, Silvia G. 2002. *Etnicidades en la costa ecuatoriana.* Quito, Ecuador: Abya Yala.

Bazurco, Martín. 2006. *«Yo soy más indio que tú»: Resignificando la etnicidad. Exploración teórica e introducción al proceso de reconstrucción étnica en las Comunas de Santa Elena, Ecuador.* Quito, Ecuador: Abya Yala.

Bruner, Jerome. 1990. *Acts of meaning.* Cambridge, Mass.: Harvard University Press.

Comaroff, Jean & John. 1992. The colonization of consciousness. In John & Jean Comaroff (eds.): *Ethnography and the historical imagination.* Boulder, Colorado: Westview Press.

Estrada, Jenny. 2001. *Ancón en la historia petrolera del Ecuador 19111976.* Guayaquil, Ecuador: ESPOL.

Friedman, Jonathan. 1994. History and the politics of identity. In Jonathan Friedman (ed.): *Cultural identity and global processes.* London: Sage Publications, s.117–146.

Johansen, Anders. 1988. Mytiske landskap. *Profil,* No. 2.

Labov, W. (1982). Speech actions and reactions in personal narrative. In Deborah Tannen (ed.): *Analyzing discourse: Text and talk.* Washington D. C.: Georgetown University Press, s. 219–247

Marcos, Jorge et al. 2004. *Las Albarradas en la Costa del Ecuador. Rescate del conocimiento ancestral del manejo sostenible de la biodiversidad.* Guayaquil, Ecuador: CEAA/ESPOL.

Selverston, Melina H. 1994. The politics of culture: indigenous peoples and the state in Ecuador. In Donna Lee van Cott (ed.): *Indigenous peoples and democracy in Latin America.* New York: St. Martin Press, pp. 131–152.

Part II

Introduction Part II: Bolivia: The Politics of Water

John-Andrew McNeish

In contrast to the previous section on Ecuador, the following section on Bolivia does not focus on the history and possibilities of any one local technology for water collection or conservation. Instead the chapters included here aim to highlight the broader political context of water as a local and national natural resource, and the impact of contrasting management strategies on social development. Whilst previous studies (Swanley 2002) of indigenous knowledge in Bolivia have characterised the existence of local water and land management techniques, such as the *suko-kullo* (raised fields), the studies included here emphasise the politics of knowledge that surround them and the importance of natural resources as an issue of not only local concern, but of national debate and stability.

Bolivia has been the scene of a series of violent confrontations between the government and a range of social interest groups over the last few years. These confrontations led to a chain of events including a state of emergency, a rising death toll amongst protesters, the burning of government buildings and the resignation of two national Presidents. With these confrontations foreign investments in the country were placed in question, enterprises and tourists left the country and the country's national economy was left in crisis. However, whilst damaging in the short term for the nation's stability, in the course of this political and economic crisis new political opportunities and movements were born. The years of protest were also responsible for the formation of a platform for political change that ultimately led to the rupture of a pre-existing elitist political culture, and the election at the end of 2005 of Evo Morales Ayma. Morales is an Aymaran indigenous leader (i.e. one of the country's previously marginalised indigenous majority) of the country's coca growers association and leading representative of the Movement for Socialism (MAS). Key to the new political platform introduced by Morales and his supporters are recent efforts to question the conditions of the country's pre-existing neoliberal economic model, to restructure the state through the creation of a new and all-inclusive Constitutional Assembly[34] and to rethink the country's natural resource management. In connection with this last point, the Morales government have announced legislation that re-nationalises the production of oil and gas in the country, re-distributes over 20,000 hectares of land to low-income families, and places control over water services back in the hands of local communities by ending contracts signed with international concessions[35].

Although none of the current chapters are directly concerned with an explanation of the crisis and recent changes in Bolivia, they reinforce the importance of previous failures to decide on an equitable and socially sensitive model for natural resource management as key to their cause. The chapters included here highlight how it is that contrasting notions of identity, gender, modernity and culture expressed through different local, national and international development management strategies produce conflict. Here water is transformed from its neutral elements into a symbol and expression of highly contrasting and controversial ontologies, ideologies and ideas. In «Negotiating Masculinities in the Water Sector» Nina Laurie explores how gendered representations and language help to structure development discourses, and as such play a role in both the consolidation and critique of accepted understandings of development orthodoxy. In «The Politics of Shortage: Political Mobilization and Community Water Management in the Popular Neighborhoods of El Alto, Bolivia» Frank Poupeau characterizes the basis and bases of the 2004 protests against the consortium water company, Aguas de Illimani, in El Alto, Bolivia. In «When the Solution of Irrigation became a Problem» Pablo Regalsky highlights the serious social consequences that can occur as a result of the careless introduction of new micro irrigation technologies.

In highlighting the sensitivity of the ideas and practices that surround water and the need for a careful consideration of differing local circumstances the chapters in this section can be further read as containing important lessons for current Bolivian policy-makers interested in effective and acceptable government. Despite the existence of new context in which a renewed emphasis has been placed on participation in government, there remain serious concerns amongst many Bolivian social movements that an over emphasis on securing national governance could once again result in the formation of templates for development that ignore local interests and environmental concerns. At present these concerns are particularly focused on the process leading up to the formation of the new Constitutional Assembly and current discussions and debates over the formation and meaning of «autonomies». Over the last decade, there have been shifts within Bolivia to decentralising power – the law of popular participation in 1994 decentralised many funds and responsibilities to municipal level; in December 2005 there were elections for Prefects for the first time. Just as wider local government reforms produced opportunities and reasons for protest, these changes also created the

---

34. Elections for this Assembly will be held on the 2nd of June this year, in which 255 members will be elected, of which 210 will be elected by direct vote. The new constituent assembly that is formed by these elections will begin to meet on the 6th of August in Sucre, the country's «constitutional capital», and will have six months to a year to draw up the new constitution, which will be voted on by Bolivians in a referendum within 120 days of its completion.
35. For more on the Bolivian crisis see Lazar & McNeish (eds) 2005; Crabtree 2005; Albro 2005.

grounds for autonomy to be raised as a demand by regional interests. In the last few years, the Civic Committee of Santa Cruz and the Association of Industries, Commerce, Services and Tourism of Santa Cruz (CAINCO) have led a vigorous campaign including petitions and marches in favour of autonomy. With its development of large-scale soya production and agro-industry, as well as the discovery of oil and gas, elite and business interests in the Department of Santa Cruz see autonomy as a means to secure control over existing resources and profits. Similar demands have come from Tarija, Beni and Pando. In May and June 2005, Santa Cruz pro-autonomy groups added to pressure on President Mesa at the time of the gas protests by threatening to self-convene a referendum on autonomy.

Although bitterly opposed to the elite and business interests of the Santa Cruz lobby the idea of regional autonomies has, nonetheless, been accepted by the current MAS controlled government. Indeed, the recent Bill for the Creation of the Constituent Assembly not only stipulates that the election of «plurinominal» (i.e. department-wide) candidates, but that a referendum on the governmental autonomy of the departments be held at the same time as elections to the Constituent Assembly[36]. The problem with this idea of autonomy and MAS's efforts to ensure their control of it, is that the social movements responsible for the recent protests and bases of the new government share a very different conception of the meaning of autonomy – rhetorically an autonomy of the bases, and not of the «elites». Rather than defining autonomy in terms of existing departmental governments, the conceptualisation of autonomy supported by indigenous peoples and peasant farmers aims to break with existing administrative structures and to propose an idea that goes beyond a concern with territorial control to a concern with self-determination i.e. respect for the autonomy of rights and culture, and with this respect for local ideas, technologies and forms of natural resource management.

Taking this context in account, the chapters in this section further remind us then of the persisting need in Bolivia, but also existing local possibilities and limitations, for substantive participation in development strategies. Indeed, they highlight the importance that water, along with other natural resources, continues to have not only as a vital element of subsistence, but as a vital field of social and political inter-action and practice.

---

36. The question agreed by the Congress for this referendum reads: Are you in favor of, in the framework of national unity, giving the Constituent Assembly the binding power to establish autonomous departmental governments applicable inmediately after the promulgation of the new Constitution in the departments in which this referendum got the majority of votes in the manner in which its authorities are elected directly by the citizens and receive from the state executive competencies, administrative and normative attributions and the necessary economic and financial resources assigned to them by the new Constitution?

Bibliography

Albro, R. (2005) 'The Water is Ours, Carajo! Deep Citizenship in Bolivia's Water War', in Nash (ed.) *Social Movements: An Anthropological Reader*. Blackwell Publishing: London, 249–271.

Crabtree, J. (2005) *Patterns of Protest: Politics and Social Movements in Bolivia*. LAB: London

Lazar, S & McNeish, J eds (2005) *The Millions Return: Democracy in Bolivia at the Start of the 21st Century*. Special Edition. Bulletin of Latin American Research. April. Vol 25: 2

Swartley (L) *Inventing Indigenous Knowledge: Archaeology, Rural Development and the Raised Fields Rehabilitation Project in Bolivia*. Routledge: NY & London.

Establishing Development Orthodoxy: Negotiating Masculinities in the Water Sector[37]

Nina Laurie

Abstract

Despite important work in development studies on the 'male bias in the development process', it is generally recognized that gender and development analyses have been slow to engage with masculinities. Focusing attention on the nexus between identity and globalizing development discourses, this paper explores the relationship between masculinities and development through an analysis of the gendering of water paradigms. By analyzing the example of the recent Cochabamba water wars in Bolivia, and placing them in historical context, I explore how gendered representations and language are used to downplay and upgrade particular understandings of modernity as they relate to water management. I examine the mechanisms through which specific gendered identities become associated with the most successful versions of 'modern' development.

Introduction

More than two decades of mainstreaming gender into development research and policy have failed to come to grips with the masculine subject. The shift from a focus on Women In Development (WID) to Gender And Development (GAD) in the mid 1980s (Rathgeber, 1990) usefully focused attention on gendered power relations and gener-

---

37. Acknowledgements: I would like to thank Simon Marvin, Carlos Crespo and Pamela Calla who helped shaped the arguments here. Thanks too are owed to Linda Peake and three anonymous reviewers who commented very helpfully on earlier drafts. Fieldwork was funded by the Department for International Development/British Council Higher Education link on gender and development between Newcastle and San Simón University and the Economic and Social Research Council project grant L21 425 202 (1999). An earlier version of this paper was published in Development and Change 36 (3) 527-549 (2005).

ated questions about the role of identity formation in development processes. While 'male bias', as defined by Elson (1995)[38] has been extensively examined in this literature, the masculine identities in which this bias is embodied, remain largely unexamined, despite a small and growing body of work on masculinities and development, much of which has appeared in special issues of journals (see Cornwall and White, 2000; Jackson, 2000; Sweetman, 1997).

Work on the influence of male bias on gender roles, institutional cultures and development discourse has largely focused on the female subject. As a result, attention to the social exclusion of women, the feminization of poverty and women as female heads of households has become well established, examining female agency and exploring how constructions of femininities are constrained and overturned in different contexts. Changing gender identities have also been examined in relation to social movements, economic and political restructuring and in the wider context of globalization. Changing masculinities, however, have yet to be investigated to the same degree. While intending to question the silence around masculinities, this paper is not aiming to 'add men back into the development process', individual men and changing constructions of masculinities are not the focus here. Rather, my emphasis on masculine subjectivities (that is, gendered development actor identities which have political meaning) represents a renewed call to examine male bias at an ideological, institutional and discursive level.

Here I focus on the role that 'gendered terms' and 'gendered language' play in the creation of male bias. I argue that these languages help structure development discourses and consolidate accepted understandings of development orthodoxy. I explore the relationship between gendered language and development orthodoxy through a specific example of changing water paradigms. I have chosen this focus because water management has witnessed some of the greatest and most rapid development shifts in recent years and has introduced new actors onto the development scene. Debates on water also played a significant role in shaping the emphasis on gender roles in WID discourse by highlighting women's roles in water management. Considered to be the most essential basic need, access to water is a highly emotive subject. In development debates on food security, disease control and economic development water plays a central role. For some it is a gift form the gods, for others, a scarce resource that needs to be managed. As such water structures socio-cultural understandings of the world and underpins economic modes of production. It is therefore often the cause of political conflict and frequently linked to rights based and identity struggles. Therefore this paper calls for a gender analysis of water to move beyond gender roles in order to takes these factors into account.

In the first section I review the nascent literature on masculinities and development relating this to emerging water paradigms. Next, I examine shifts in water paradigms in gendered terms through an in-depth case study of an emblematic anti-water privatization movement, the Cochabamba water wars in Bolivia[39]. This, now famous, uprising in April 2000 was against a private water consortium, Aguas de Tunari, headed by

---

38. «bias that operates in favour of men as a gender, and against women as a gender.... The proximate cause of male bias in development outcomes can be analysed in terms of male bias in everyday attitudes and actions, in theoretical reasoning, and in public policy» (Elson 1995: 3-7).

Anglo-American and Bolivian interests. It is an important focus of analysis because it represented the first example of a Third World resistance movement ousting an international water company and reversing water privatization measures. The fact that the US parent company is now suing the Bolivian government for breach of contract indicates the important role that this case study is playing in shaping debates over the ethics of privatization and water governance globally.

Despite the mushrooming of popular and academic work on the Cochabamba water wars[40], much of this work, to date, has focused on the moment of the uprising itself, failing to place the Cochabamba water wars in wider historical perspective. Instead, researchers have tended to emphasize a social movement analysis questioning whether the Co-ordinator (La Coordinadora), the cross alliance of professionals (including engineers), peasant and indigenous activists, irrigators, unions and women's organizations that led the wars, represents the alternative non-partisan, political institutions associated with New Social Movements (Crespo, 2000). The way in which this movement 'jumped scale' and accessed and shaped transnational anti-globalization networks has also been a topic of discussion. Very little work, however, has examined the gender dimensions of the uprisings.

In this paper I focus on how masculinities have been constructed, evoked and negotiated in the struggle over water privatization in Cochabamba from the mid 1990s. I do this in order to illustrate how particular approaches towards water management, adopted by specific interest groups, become explicitly gendered through time as struggles over establishing development orthodoxy take place. I argue that while development studies are beginning to grapple with masculinities, the subject categories currently available for understanding the relationship between development and masculinities are limiting. Representations of masculinities as heroic, vulnerable and/or oppressive, as discussed below, are too fixed. Rather than argue for extending the list of categories, however, in this paper I prioritize political agency by using a language of gendered subjectivities that focuses on struggles between development actors that invoke issues of identity. The conclusion highlights the need to expand understandings of masculinity in development studies. I call for more work to explore the diverse masculine subjectivities emerging through globalization and examine the role of gender discourses in framing successful development imaginaries.

---

39. This case study draws on fieldwork conducted as part of three larger projects on water privatisation, gender and development and indigenous politics. The 1995 data are draw from 16 semi-structured interviews with water utilities, donor/government agencies and water activists conducted jointly with Professor Simon Marvin. October 1999 – January 2000 involved extensive personal participant observation in activist meetings, protests, road blocks and the Misicuni dam company and more than 20 informal and semi-structured interviews. Follow up fieldwork in June and December 2001 and April 2002 included 3 semi-structured interviews with Coordinadora leaders. All interviews were taped and transcribed and accompanied by extensive archive research (government documents and newspaper sources).
40. See Crespo (2003), Laserna (2000), Laurie et al. (2002), Shultz (2002), Vargas and Kruse (2000) Nickson and Vargas (2002).

The masculine subject in development and water

Increasingly, research is beginning to address the influence of development processes on masculinities and, to a lesser extent, examine the ways in which particular masculinities themselves influence the types of development that take place. Development discourses and practices in all sectors, including water, seem to be becoming increasingly similar across the world, as international donors globalize understandings of best practice in their support for variations upon a neo-liberal development model.

Work on globalization is beginning to examine masculinities through research that seeks to identify the connections between macro-economic processes and processes of embodiment. This work examines the different types of 'people', 'identities' and 'bodies' that become associated with specific political and economic processes and policies (Youngs 2000). Drawing on Connell's (1995) notion of competing masculinities, Hooper (2000a) argues that the way we experience globalization in any place reflects specific and competing notions of masculinity, femininity and gender relations. She suggests that:

> *(T)he discourse of globalization itself becomes one site ... [for] gendered interpretative struggles as the meaning of globalization is contested. In the process, different «elements» or ingredients of masculinity and femininity are co-opted in new or old configurations to serve particular interests, and particular gendered (and other) identities are consolidated and legitimated or downgraded and devalued. This involves power struggles between men and women, but also between different groups of men as they jostle for position and control; articulating and re-articulating the relationship between masculinity and power as they go. (Hooper 2000a:60)*

While seemingly all pervasive, globalizing and homogenizing understandings of development policy are nonetheless increasingly being questioned. This is particularly evident when bi-lateral and multi-lateral donor organizations attempt to respond to the problems of 'male bias' and the feminization and indigenization of poverty with approaches that emphasize social development and development with identity (Davis, 2002). Under such paradigms culture (and therefore identity) are seen as a resource rather than an impediment to development (Laurie et al., 2003) and debates about the agency of diverse development actors are opened up, albeit sometimes unwittingly.

Much of the new social emphasis in development policy has emerged through Gender and Development (GAD) 'Adjustment with a Human Face' (Jolly 1991) critiques of the social costs of the harsh neo-liberal adjustment policies in the 1980s (see Regalsky, this volume, for a dramatic example of such costs for women in a Bolivian rural society). The modified neo-liberal approaches that have subsequently emerged have, in turn, provided a new terrain for the contestation of globalization and development orthodoxy in a range of fields including the water sector. In water management the introduction of a social agenda has meant increased debate over indigenous water rights and user identity (Laurie et al 2002), user decision making and participation in network extension and the use of pro-poor criteria in monitoring private sector investment in urban water utilities (Laurie and Crespo 2003).

The focus on a social, pro-poor agenda together with critiques of GAD's failure to engage with masculinities, has led to an emerging body of work on masculinities much of which adopts well established Gender and Development forms of analysis such as changing household gender relations and gendered divisions of work (see Jackson 2000). This research disaggregates understandings of gender and examines the ways in which masculinity is constructed, re-constructed and cut across by differences of generation, ethnicity, class and sexuality. A range of masculine subjects are appearing in this literature most of which are scaled at the levels of the nation state, local communities and/or the household rather than making direct links between these and the global scale of development policy making mentioned above.

First, 'heroic' masculinities are being identified through historical analyses of resistance struggles, focused on alternative national development imaginaries in different contexts. In Latin America Calla (1996) examines the importance of heroic, charismatic and legal-rational masculinities in the Nicaraguan revolution, while De la Cadena (2000) reveals the role played by heroic regional masculinities in national power broking in Peru in the early 20th Century. These analyses focus on the importance of constructions of 'heroic' masculinities in successful and geographically bounded resistance struggles. Such an approach has been extended to successful water struggles as part of the social movements analyses. I shall return to, and develop this point further, in the discussion of the Cochabamba water wars below.

In contrast to representations of heroic masculinities the 'vulnerable man' is emerging as a second important masculine subject in the development literature. One of the most highly visible vulnerable masculinities in the development literature is the 'vulnerable indigenous man'. Associated with the embodiment of poverty through numerous studies and development reports, indigenous people represent the 'poorest of the poor' in almost every development indicator. Representations of indigenous people as poor feminized indigenous people (men and women) pervade in development discourses (Radcliffe et al. forthcoming). Just as welfare rhetorics have served to devalue and diminish women's contributions to development (Tinker, 1990), discourses of poverty have marginalized and typecast indigenous livelihoods as 'backwards', 'non-modern' and 'poor'. Women's involvement in poverty alleviation is termed 'welfarist' and an extension of domestic roles. Indigenous men's association with poverty is also similarly feminized. They are cast as vulnerable subjects and the targets of alleviation programs.

In the water sector a vulnerable image of indigenous people (feminized men and women) is often invoked in environmental debates over proposed 'techno-fix' mega projects. The International Commission report on Dams (2000) gives much attention to indigenous people and highlights the negative impact of large dams on indigenous livelihoods. International environmental campaign, especially those working through the internet, however, have been criticized for sometimes reproducing vulnerable indigenous stereotypes and feminizing and anonymizing indigenous voices (Laurie 1999).

A third masculine subject emerging in the development literature, the violent oppressor, potentially gives a new structural adjustment twist to an old feminist tale. In Bolivia Calla and Rojas (1998) explores how structural adjustment during the 1980's affected masculinities. Due to large-scale mine closures men, who became out of work miners, were obliged to dedicate their time to small (informal) economic activities while women had to incorporate themselves into the labour market in large numbers. Men could no longer 'produce, provide and protect' as they used to, much in the same way that the State could no loner fulfil a similar paternal role under neo-liberal adjustment[41]. This situation triggered a crisis where the family became the last bastion of authority and many men ended up imposing violent authoritarian control over the household. In such times of structural change, gender relations often come to focus on negotiating and managing oppressor masculinities. Gill's (2000) work on masculinities and the military after the return to democracy in Bolivia also examines changes in the violent male subject and illustrates the complex relationship between development, nation building and masculinity through which social and political change is forged. The emphasis on negotiating masculinities in transition is particularly important in the discussion of water in Bolivia where the introduction of privatization and its resistance has been influenced by the memory of government under the authoritarian dictatorship of Hugo Banzer (1971–78) and successive coups during the 1980s.

In the next section these masculine subjects are examined in relation to the water privatization debate in Bolivia. I explain and contextualize the water privatization process and analyze how Bolivian water politics have responded to global shifts in water management. I explore how recent paradigm shifts in water management have produced new development actors and challenged the power and positions of established experts, institutions and knowledges. The second section moves onto a gendered analysis of the struggles involved in fixing understandings of globalization in the water sector through the case study of the privatization debate in Cochabamba from the mid 1990s.

Bolivia in the new water paradigm

Water management is currently one of the most rapidly globalizing industries. Publicly owned municipal water companies are increasingly an anachronism as a small number of international water companies come to dominate water markets across the world (Hall 1999). This is largely a North-South relationship as companies with origins in Europe and the US comprise the core of the transnational water business. Models of privatization in countries of the North, such as the UK (Bakker 2000), have been exported to the South and newly privatized Northern companies have 'gone global'.

These markets and companies largely owe their rapid growth to the recent shift by international donor organizations towards supporting privatization. Supporters of privatization argue that state-owned water companies are over staffed, inefficient institutions open to political interference and are therefore unable to invest in providing clean water for the poor (Nickson, 2001). While variations on the privatization model exist (Public Private Partnerships, and the granting of concessions for limited time periods – see Hall, 2000) the basic principal is that only with private sector investment and the restructuring and stripping down of personnel can more effective services be delivered.

The Bolivia water scene has mirrored global shifts in recent years. In the 1990s, under the Sanchez de Losada government, a series of privatizations occurred across a

---

41. I am grateful to Pamela Calla for bringing my attention to this work.

range of sectors (Kohl, 2002) supported by World Bank loans for institutional strengthening in order to prepare public companies for sale. Water came onto the agenda in the mid 1990s and centred on the facilities in Cochabamba and La Paz-El Alto (Laurie and Marvin, 1999), which up until this point, had functioned as publicly owned municipal companies reflecting the types of water service found in most large Latin American cities from the 1950s onwards.

In keeping with a paradigm shift away from large-scale, techno-fix solutions to water management, donor support for Misicuni, a large multiple dam complex in Cochabamba, was withdrawn in the 1990s when the World Bank and Inter American Development Bank discontinued funding for the project. Support for Misicuni, however, remained strong in the city of Cochabamba reflecting the fact that the 'Myth of Misicuni' had fuelled modernization dreams since the 1950s. Local engineers had built their careers studying its logistics and successive politician had promised to deliver the project while campaigning (Laurie and Marvin, 1999). As a result, there was much opposition to water privatization in Cochabamba as popular opinion felt that the privatization of the municipal water company, SEMAPA, would undermine plans for the Misicuni project, as a private company would not have much interest in financing a large dam. Also local government, composed largely of parties in opposition to Sanchez de Losada's government, resented central government's interference in what it considered to be municipal property and a local issue. The privatization debate over SEMAPA therefore blew up into a fully-fledged regional struggle in the mid 1990s.

Discontent with the privatization agenda in Cochabamba in 1995 coincided with a lack of interest from foreign investors in SEMAPA at this time. They were more interested in the capital city, La Paz-El Alto facility, which was financially more robust and did not have Cochabamba's water scarcity problems. Eventually, plans to privatize SEMAPA in Cochabamba were dropped by the government and the La Paz-El Alto concession was sold to a French-led consortium.

The Cochabamba water wars

Privatization came on the agenda again in Cochabamba four years later under the new administration of Hugo Banzer, the ex military dictator who was democratically elected to power after Losada's government lost the 1996 elections. A UK-led proposal from International Waters, which had formed a consortium 'Aguas de Tunari' in association with the American company Bechtel and selected Bolivian entrepreneurs, was the only company to participate in the bidding process for a 30 year concession in the city. According to the British director of Aguas de Tunari the decision to go forward with the negotiations was a courageous one on the part of the government:

> *The decision of the government to form the negotiating committee to negotiate with us after we were the only bidder was a courageous decision because it obviously opens everybody to criticism. (Author's interview with Mr. Thorpe the director of Aguas de Tunari, Cochabamba, November 1999).*

Whether brave or ill-advised, the Aguas de Tunari concession provoked outrage in Cochabamba for a number of reasons. The negotiations were shrouded in secrecy and the company was established in a tax haven normally associated in Bolivia with drug money laundering (Shultz, 2002). Controversy arose about the fact that the initial investment registered on paper by the foreign partners was ridiculously low, prompting accusations of government corruption. Distrust about government involvement was also compounded by the legislative changes associated with the Aguas de Tunari concession.

A new water and sanitation law (Law 2029) was passed hastily in the autumn of 1999 to provide the legislative framework that would allow the Aguas de Tunari concession to go ahead. Indigenous and peasant activists felt that many clauses in the law had been added in without any consultation. They argued that water commodification threatened indigenous livelihoods and rights which were recognized and protected by Bolivia's pluri-cultural constitution (Laurie et al, 2002). In particular, they felt that it would undermine the extensive network of alternative water systems operating on the peripheries of Cochabamba and delivering up to 33% of the city's water supply (Crespo 2003). These networks rely on community built infrastructure, wells, drains, irrigation systems, aqueducts and water tankers, managed by a series of social institutions based on 'uses and customs'.

Crespo (2003: 132–133) argues that '«uses and customs' practices in water are part of the reciprocity system and mutual support systems of traditional Andean society …uses and customs practices allow the constitution of water organisations, with specific rules', and are thus a significant component of a strong civil society». These water organizations comprise autonomous, non-profit water associations, co-operatives and committees which work together with neighborhood and agricultural syndicates when water rights are under threat. They operate their own norms and rules for water use and decisions are made in user assemblies. Some alternative water organizations retain rituals that thank mother earth, and a strong body of knowledge on water conservation and climate change underpins their water management strategies (Crespo 2003).

The controversy over the introduction of Law 2029 reached a climax in November 1999 when, upon taking over the concession, Aguas de Tunari announced a tariff hike and proposed locating water meters in sewerage systems in households not formally connected to the drinking water system. While the average tariff increase was thirty five per cent many households experienced rises of two hundred per cent. These rises and the threat that the imposition of meters in alternative systems represented to the symbolic relations of uses and customs, were the final straw for many people in Cochabamba. They argued that, as a cultural practice, these uses and customs can be traced back to pre-Colombian times and should therefore be respected. The argument was not that the alternative systems themselves were necessarily old (although some of them date back hundreds of years), but that the practice of 'uses of customs' represents cultural heritage and forms a key part of civil society. Therefore, if threatened, citizens had the right to call for the protection of this heritage in a pluri-cultural nation. In this way, the call to protect uses and customs is a direct appeal to the neo-liberal development with identity stance on socially inclusive, culturally sensitive progress and modernity. In terms of current 'pro-poor' water paradigms, it is also an appeal by poor users to have their rights to participate in decision-making processes recognized.

Initial protests against Aguas de Tunari started in November 1999 and after a series of strikes, marches and road blocks throughout the department of Cochabamba, culminated in the Cochabamba water wars and a violent stand off with Banzer's government in April 2000 (Laurie et al., 2002). The outcome was a victory for the Cochabamba protestors. The government nullified the concession contract with Aguas de Tunari, the company withdrew and SEMAPA returned. Subsequently, Law 2029 was replaced with Law 2066 that recognizes uses and customs and the legal standing of alternative water systems.

While accepting that New Social Movements approaches in the social sciences have been widely critiqued[42], it is important to acknowledge that, at different moments, the Cochabamba water wars represented new alliances across class, gender and ethnicity. Middle, peasant and urban-working class individuals and organizations joined together in the protests. The Coordinadora leadership, drawn from professionals, unions and women's organizations among others, had support from both mestizo (mixed race) and indigenous Quechua groups. These alliances ruptured the rural/urban dichotomy that characterizes politics in many countries of the South and introduced new political subjects. Most importantly, the uses and customs platform challenged the often essentialized, pauperised representations of indigenous actors located in rural space by showing that uses and customs are relevant in the city and that urban and middle class Bolivians could claim indigenous cultural heritage (Laurie et al., 2002).

In the following section I shall analyze these new political subjects in relation to the gendered development discourses underlying Bolivian water politics from 1995 to 2000. The main argument will be that to understand what has happened in the recent Cochabamba water wars analyses must go beyond an 'a' historic, new social movement celebration of alliances across difference. Instead, the focus needs to be on examining the ways in which development paradigms about water have become gendered. I will argue that modernization, as reinvented through neo-liberal water policies, is sustained by rivalries between different development discourses embodied in specific masculine subjectivities that are differentially privileged and marginalized through processes of scale. The case of Cochabamba is examined in detail in order to illustrate that these power relationships are not fixed and that hegemonic masculine subjectivities associated with globalization can be contested from, and constructed in the South, as well as, the North.

Whose Modern? The role of gendered language in creating development orthodoxy

Hooper (2000a) argues that the way we experience globalization in any place reflects a set of competing masculinities as different groups of men jostle for position and control, shaping the relationship between masculinity and power in the process. I would argue that this positioning also influences the definitions of appropriate development that become established through globalization processes. The emergence of the 'Coor-

---

42. For example, critics highlight the failure of this literature to see continuities with past movements, for over exaggerating the non-partisan nature of new institutions and creating iconoclastic stereotypes of super heroes, especially women (Laurie with Calla, in press).

dinadora' in Cochabamba reflects a reaction to the historical downgrading and devaluing of particular and competing Bolivian expressions of development. These expressions of development become gendered in relation to the dominant masculinity and form of power that is embodied in globalization processes. Thus, while the Cochabamba water war was fought over issues of cost and ways of life, it was also about particular and different versions of 'the modern' that emerged through the privatization debate and the development actor identities that were able successfully to become associated with them.

Various authors argue that conceptualizations of gender and specific gender relations and identities form part of the 'social epistemology' (assumptions and forms of thinking about society) of a given era (Connell, 1995). Hooper (2000b) asserts that the modern capitalist era, where globalization is of paramount importance, is formed in part by bourgeois rational masculinity and the rational actor model:

> «By this is meant that there are deep qualitative differences between each era or epoch in history, differences which span not only social, political and economic organization, but also philosophy, psychology and subjectivity. Not only are such arrangements different from one era to the next, but within each era there is a dominant social epistemology, so that recurring assumptions and patterns tend to cross all disciplinary boundaries. (Hooper, 2000b: 42)

While Hooper's argument about the relationship between the social epistemology of late global capitalism and the maintenance of the position of the bourgeois masculine subject is important, there is a tendency for such interpretations to assume that an 'era' is geographically uniform and uncontested. In a postcolonial context such as Bolivia, late capitalism is far from consolidated and what is at stake is which actors and identities can best associate themselves with the most 'successful' (in representational terms) definition of the most 'modern' development approach. While Hooper (2000b) and Connell (1995) suggest that an era can define qualitative differences in the social epistemology, in postcolonial contexts different versions of modernity co-exist and compete, therefore a specific era is neither clear cut nor is the dominant social epistemology consolidated. The legacies of colonialism, republicanism and the neo-colonialism of contemporary North/South development relations configure the experience of late capitalism. These power relations frame the politics that came to be played out in the Cochabamba water wars and the privatization debates that led up to them.

In Bolivia 'modernization' has only ever been partial in its coverage and uptake, yet dreams of modernization (embodied in the case of Cochabamba in support for the Misicuni project) still drive many development goals (Laurie and Marvin, 1999). While water privatization and commodification is being pushed by the State, the same State is also engaged in recognizing the rights of indigenous groups to self determination and collective land owning under a pluri-cultural constitution (Laurie et al., 2002). These two agendas are often not compatible, adding to further competition between different versions of modernity and definitions of what constituted the 'most modern' approach towards development.

Competition over defining modernity can become gendered; feminized and masculinized, in different ways as specific positions, and the interest groups associated with them, seek to establish their visions of development as hegemonic. The gendering of competing versions of modernity, progress and development is clearly evident in water management.

In Bolivia three gendered versions of 'the modern' ('Technocratic neoliberalism', social development and 'techno-fix development') have become associated with water since privatization first came on to the agenda in the early 1990s. These gender and often racially marked definitions of 'modern development' compete through processes of subordination and domination as global understandings of neo-liberal development become established in development discourses, institutions and funding policies. In Bolivia political positioning has taken place in response to the tensions created by donor and State attempts to consolidate a new orthodoxy about water.

The emasculated subject and the global policing of technocratic neo-liberalism

The rise of a new class of technocrats charged with implementing democratization is a hallmark of neo-liberal development (Silva, 1998). Technocratic neo-liberal development has implications for the public sector in countries of the South. Focusing on institutional change and down-sizing as part of wider economic adjustment, financial efficiency has become the goal of a new technocratic, managerial science.

Supported by donors and usually included as a pre-requisite in debt relief programs 'institutional change' often reflects thinly disguised neo-colonial assumptions about the relationship between inefficiency and pervasive corruption in the South. Institutional strengthening plans, such as those funded for the water sector in Bolivia, prior to the first round of water privatization, generate resentment among the 'old' mestizo public sector class of technocrats staffing municipal institutions like water companies. For example, the former director of SEMAPA Cochabamba resented the fact that the use of foreign consultants (usually white, Northern men) to run institutional strengthening programs questioned his management skills and integrity.

> «*The World Bank funded a program of institutional strengthening for the water company to improve the directorship, administration and the operations maintenance of the installations. ... They contracted a (foreign) consultant to do the work for this. .... This is because they believed that we wanted to hide some insufficiency.*» (Author's interview with the former director of SEMAPA, Cochabamba, December 1995).

The importation of foreign consultants for these programs points to the unequal competition that globalization processes have generated for Southern public sector development actors. In this case, the Bolivian development actor identities embodied in public sector technocrats are given no voice. Despite their in-depth knowledge of the company and local context an outside 'expert' is imposed upon the municipal company from above. This imposition cannot be challenged as it is the condition for outside aid. The knowledge and expertise of the local manager is downgraded and this local/regional Cochabamban and Bolivian development actor is 'emasculated'; left powerless. Accusations of corruption are implied and a transnational expert polices the company activities and managers with authority from the World Bank and the La Paz based government. In this scenario privatization becomes a punishment for (mis)management, corruption and inefficiency and local technocrats become 'victims' as they lose their jobs and their companies. The public sector development paradigms that they represent loose status, become outdated and are marginalized.

The feminized subject and the social development agenda

Associated with the global shift away from techno-fix solutions to development has been the rise of a user focused, social development agenda in water management. The latest development thought suggests that systems are better designed, better maintained and better sustained if users are involved. Borrowing largely from NGO experience with community participation in alternative water systems, donors are increasingly encouraging user involvement as part of a pro-poor agenda. In this way the provision of water systems can become part of enhancing the social capital of poor communities through their participation in the provision and maintenance of systems in emblematic private sector 'pro-poor' initiatives. A key example is the La Paz-El Alto concession which is well publicized by the World Bank (Komvives 1999).

Despite the positive publicity around private sector social development initiatives, the long-standing legacies of public sector participation in pro-poor water provision is not respected to the same degree in privatization debates. Rather, the association of a municipal water company with a social development agenda is seen as welfarist. The subjects involved are poor people living on the peripheries of the city, who are often indigenous, rural migrants. They are seen as vulnerable, and thus, the social development agenda is seen as welfarist and 'feminized. It is downgraded as noncommercial, as the example of representations of SEMAPA's participation program in 1995 illustrates.

Throughout the 1990s SEMAPA ran a water education program with poor communities in Cochabamba. This program received extensive funding from FIS (Fondo de Inversion Social) the Social Investment Fund in Bolivia, the leading government social development unit in the 1990s. This fund invested in infrastructure provision and emphasized the use and training of community labor. Gender approaches were mainstreamed and workshops, videos and radio programs were produced as part of its integrated education program working to extend the water network into poor neighborhoods.

> «The important thing in the training programs that were developed is that the whole family participated because if only the man, woman or children (were to) participate there is no integrated education.»(Author's interview with the water training program co-ordinator working for SEMAPA funded by FIS, Cochabamba November 1995)

Despite SEMAPA's obvious success in fulfilling social development criteria and spear heading the latest thinking on community development and access to water, private sector investors downgraded these initiatives because they were not commercial.

«We would go to the poorest neighborhood and ask for $80 to connect households to the network ... this (new connections for the poor) was not the problem. The problem was that we had to have an efficient company (and that meant) of course you had to improve the participation of the private sector.» (Author's interview with the former director of SEMAPA, Cochabamba, December 1995)

«Obviously the people from the water company argued that they had international aid and that they also gave a social function to the provision of drinking water but that was not enough.» (Author's interview with a Bolivian entrepreneur participating in the first round of water privatization – La Paz, December, 1995)

Despite carrying out some of the most 'modern' forms of water management SEMAPA's social development agenda was marginalized because it was not market oriented. It was downgraded by association with a welfare (feminized) agenda, not matter how cutting edge its methods and goals were.

The marginalized masculine subject – techno-fix development and subordinated engineers

With the advent of an emerging new development orthodoxy on water management a whole generation of civil engineers have been obliged to 're-tool'. In countries of the South this has perhaps been more difficult than in the North. In the South the hard science of engineering has been celebrated throughout the drive towards modernization from the 1950s onwards. This (nearly always) masculine subject became a hero of national and regional development dreams, gaining respect and authority. Wielding political power with techno-fix solutions to poverty and mega-project short cuts to a more modern society, it is no coincidence that leading politicians and in some cases presidents have been drawn from the ranks of civil engineers.

The globalization of the water industry therefore dealt a double blow to such masculine subjects, not only was their expertise and professional knowledge questioned, but also along with this they lost their standing and legitimacy in national development agendas. Globalization has meant that, increasingly, water management decisions are being taken at another scale by transnational companies, legitimated and directed by foreign consultants. In Bolivia the international consultant firm Dames and More played an important role in de-legitimating the Misicuni proposal which many local engineers have spent the best part of their careers studying and supporting. Thus, Southern nationals have been ousted from engineering leadership under the new scenario, vulnerable victims of global restructuring.

Such shifts, however, have not gone uncontested. In the first round of privatization discussions in 1995 these marginalized Bolivian experts attempted to re-assert their position. In Cochabamba the head of the Civil Engineers Society at the time, Gonzalo Maldonado (who later become a parliamentarian and a prominent figure in the Coordinadora during the water wars) actively questioned the legitimacy of foreign experts.

«Well not all of the information is correct. It isn't adequate because there are some data about well borings that are not complete. So [the image of the company that will

> be privatized] is not really very real. They [foreign consultants] have prepared this [consultancy report] so that foreigners become potential investors. The companies that come to see the water company need to see a company that's doing ok so that it gives a good impression.» (Author's interview with the head of the engineer's organization who later became a senator and key figure in the Coordinadora, Cochabamba, November, 1995)

Even the director of FIS in Cochabamba had doubts about the ways in which statistics were being produced to package a public company in order to attract private investors:

> «The percentage (of the population connect to the water network) is a marvelous mechanism for the bidding process. In accordance with what you need you can get a percentage of anything!» (Author's interview with the head FIS, Cochabamba, December, 1995)

More importantly, in the context of the water wars that were to follow 1999–2000, was the attempt by Bolivian marginalized professionals to use their expertise as a rallying call for popular protest.

> «The only thing we see to do as a solution for this country is organize the citizens. To begin with we need people with the right criteria (engineers) who can organize and give them the technical criteria to be able to protest with the technological know-how necessary.» (Author's interview with the head of the engineer's organization who later became a senator and key figure in the Coordinadora, Cochabamba, November, 1995)

With such a call, Bolivian engineers were attempting to reassert the place of national expertise in globalization and to re-insert themselves as heroic, 'expert' subjects into the regional and national development imaginaries that they were being excluded from.

From marginal to heroic 'alternative' hegemonic masculine subjectivities

In 1995 the leadership of the Cochabamba anti-privatization protests was embodied in marginalized masculinities trying to become heroic again. While the voices of the engineers, union activists and public sector technocrats were raised, the mayor of Cochabamba, Manfred Villa Reyes became the hero of the 1995 resistance movement. Villa Reyes, previously a captain in the army, waged a personal political battle against president Sanchez de Losada and his privatization measures. With the return of the military to the barracks, as outlined by Gill (2000), Villa Reyes position in opposition to the government of Sanchez de Losada can be seen as an expression of a new style of military political leadership in democratic times. It is also a more contemporary example of De la Cadena's (2000) analysis of the assertion of regional masculinities in national power broking. Manfred Reyes came to embody the marginal power of 'the local' and 'the regional' in the context of globalization and successfully resisted the centralizing power of the La Paz based government as it sought, with World Bank support, to globalize Bolivian water markets.

When the former military dictator, Victor Hugo Banzer, replaced Losada's administration the heroic return of the military masculine subject to (democratic) political power was completed. However, when four years later the Cochabamba water wars provoked an authoritarian military response from Banzer's government, it became clear that the military masculine subject was not fully reformed by democracy. The use of soldiers and military force to quell wide-spread public protest was more reminiscent of Banzer's earlier dictatorship than his more recent experience of elected rule. The violence of the repression suggests a failure in (democratic) military masculinities. In the following section I discuss how these failures were not the only masculinities to influence the conflict. I identify the failure of other powerful (global) masculinities and, building on approaches that focus on the importance of social movements and indigenous rights in the struggle, examine the gender dimensions of leadership, concentrating particularly on masculinities.

The failure of Northern masculine subjectivities to gain hegemony

Focusing on competing masculinities it is easy to conclude that the government lost the Cochabamba water wars because Banzer's military masculinity failed to gain hegemony. It is also possible, however, to argue that the Aguas de Tunari leadership was not flexible enough and that the masculine identity that they represented in the context of an emerging global water industry and market was not successful in establishing itself. Hooper's (2000a) discourse analysis of job adverts for top executives in *The Economist* (a leading current affairs magazine with world-wide circulation) points to how globalization becomes established by portraying particular identities and embodying specific masculine subjectivities. These subjectivities combine all that is successful in business terms about Anglo-American hegemonic masculinity (a veneer of social informality, teamwork and flexibility while pursuing competitiveness) with an attention to specificity, local culture, team learning and knowledge sharing which Hooper identifies as characterizing Asian (Japanese) business masculinities.

In Hooper's terms Aguas de Tunari did not express a fluid enough 'Asia-Anglo-American' masculine subjectivity. Their model of neo-liberal privatization lacked 'adjustment with a human face'. The tariff rises were extremely high, yet non negotiable, they stuck to a hard line, inflexible economic understanding of globalization. In contrast to Hooper's characterization of an 'Asian' attention to specific cultural context in the Anglo-American Asian hegemonic masculinity, the leaders of Aguas de Tunari failed to take the local context seriously. While several members of the leadership team took Spanish lessons, stories circulated that the company director, Mr. Thorpe, was so out of touch that he did not understand who 'La Coordinadora' was and thought the phrase referred to an individual woman, The Coordinator (la coordinadora, is a feminine noun in Spanish).

> «The head of the union had called a meeting and the technical director (of Aguas de Tunari), who was English, was there and he told them that they were visiting the

communities with the neighborhood committees. He said the neighborhood communities represented the people who were affected (by the price hikes and meters) and that they were reaching an agreement. They (Aguas de Tunari) were dispelling their doubts and preoccupations but, whatever happened, the director Mr. Thorpe wanted to dialogue with the Sra Coordinadora (Mrs. Coordinator). He had heard of the Sra Coordinadora and he wanted to meet her, could the union please bring her to him? So they explained to him that it wasn't anything to do with a lady and that La Coordinadora was an organization that had joined together to fight for the water». (Author's interview with Oscar Olivera, one of the leaders of the Coordinadora, Cochabamba, December 2000)[43].

Similarly, comments were made about the fact that Mr. Thorpe did not know that his name was pronounced 'Torpe', in Spanish, which literally translated means clumsy. Whether apocrypha or not such stories represented a huge public relations gaff for Aguas de Tunari. When the cultural history of water politics in Cochabamba was raised in an interview, the British management team cited their other global experiences:

«*Some of the technical problems we have here are similar to the Philippines. They have a shortage of water. And so the idea of control, rationing, and so on, are very similar in that respect. They're also waiting for this a dream water project to bring in water from elsewhere*». (Author's interview with Mr. Thorpe, Director of Aguas de Tunari, Cochabamba, November 1999).

For the Aguas de Tunari leadership, Cochabamba was like the Philippines, Buenos Aires and Chile where they had previously worked. They failed to take the socio-cultural context seriously and saw only the technical problems of water scarcity and the need for political negotiations with the State over the concession. They were naïve about the relationship between the granting of their concession and wider political events, seeing the launch of their concession and the passing of Law 2029 merely as 'an unfortunate coincidence', rather than as anything politically more sinister[44].

It is perhaps unsurprising that, in the context of this naivety, the subordinated Bolivian development actors who had tried to assert influence in 1995 re-emerged on the political scene.

New hybrid global heroes

The gender identities displayed by the Cochabamba Coordinadora and its supporters during the Cochabamba water wars (1999–2000) are another tale of marginalized masculinities becoming heroic. The masculine identities in the Coordinadora comprised previously marginalized engineers, public sector technocrats and the union and co-op-

---

43. This interview, also cited below, was undertaken with Pamela Calla.
44. «It's most unfortunate really that we started our contract more or less exactly the same date as the Ley de Sanamiento Basico was passed and the project of the water law was in the congress». (Mr Thorpe, Director of Aguas de Tunari, Cochabamba, November 1999)

erative leaders who had been unable to stop the successive waves of privatization that swept across Bolivia in the 1990s. The type of leadership that developed in the Coordinadora, however, appeared to be a departure from the individualistic, partisan, masculinist caudillo culture that traditionally characterizes union and party politics in Latin America. Instead, the alliances across difference that the Coordinadora represented implied a new form of consensual politics that also provided a space for with women's activism and leadership[45].

As well as the emergence of consensual masculine political subjects and a reversal in the fortunes of military masculine identities, a major difference between the heroic masculinities of 1995 and 2000 was the way in which the local heroes of Cochabamba's water wars jumped scale and came to occupy an important place in the global anti-capitalist movement. Through e-mail contacts Oscar Olivera, one of the leaders of the Coordinadora and a longstanding union activist, was invited to speak at the anti-capitalist rallies in Washington in early 2000. He emphasized the emotion he felt while speaking at the meeting:

«*They took us directly from the airport with out suitcases with nothing and we rushed because the meeting was finishing. I just started to talk as I was nervous. I just told them what had happened. There were 400 people there and they said that the whole world was affected by what I said. When I went in September and then October they said this and remembered what I had said and said that really they had been greatly affected by it. I just tried to tell them about the experiences that one had lived and tried to explain it very simply and with a lot of sentiment*». (Authors interview with Oscar Olivera one of the leaders of the Coordinadora, Cochabamba December 2001)

By speaking with emotion and sentiment, rather than merely rationality in the global public arena, the masculine subjectivity embodied by the Coordinadora leadership seemed to break down the rational/emotional dichotomy which Hooper (2000b) claims is so dear to bourgeois masculinity. While the extent to which such global constructions of bourgeois masculinities have any basis in or lasting impact on local realities remains to be examined, and questions should be raised about the degree to which any contemporary masculinity remains firmly fixed by enlightenment binaries of emotion and rationality, this quotation points to the importance of global networks in shaping development actor behaviour, identities and political influence. Globally scaled, the consensual, sensitive masculine actor that emerged through the Cochabamba water wars not only embodied the hybrid identities celebrated in the New Social Movements literature but also had much resonance in activist circles. This masculinity helped establish the Cochabamba water wars as an indigenous environmental struggle in global anti-capitalist networks. The following analysis of a solidarity visit made to Cochabamba by a Northern indigenous activist illustrates this point and raises questions about the construction of such a collective identity and the role of scale and hybridity in struggles over globalization and water.

---

45. Key positions in the Coordinadora were held by women and many women played important leadership roles locally. In areas with formal water co-operatives and water associations, women took attendance lists at blockades, imposing fines on neighbors who did not participate.

In December 2001 Chief Gary John, a First Nations leaders from British Colombia, Canada, visited Bolivia as part of a delegation sponsored by the Council of Canadians. He came to learn from the Cochabamba experience and to take his lessons North.

«If the Liberal government gets in, they say they'd privatize BC hydro and BC rail. In my community and in other communities, what that will mean is that this publicly run railroad and publicly run hydro-electric development corporation, which has been very devastating on my people [will be privatized]. Instead of us dealing with the crown corporation, we'd be dealing with a private company, we'd probably end up in the same situation as these people here…. So we'd be of no use, so if I can bring back what I've learned about globalization, about privatization, about what I can do and about what I can't do [I can help]. I can bring back that experience, that knowledge and experience [which I have gained] with the people in Cochabamba». (Author's interview with Chief Gary John, representative of First Nations Peoples in Canada, Cochabamba, December 2001).

When asked in the same interview why he had come to Cochabamba specifically, Chief Gary John said that he had wanted to meet indigenous leaders like Oscar Olivera. While the use of such a label for a mestizo, Spanish-speaking, union activist like Olivera might raise a questioning eyebrow in some quarters, in transnational protest circuits the association of indigenous identities with environmental protests has much resonance. The promotion of environmental campaigns often involves representations of conflicts as indigenous struggles.

While global environmental campaigns, especially those promoted through the web, often rest upon essentialized representations of indigenous people as femininized guardians of nature (Laurie, 1999), the masculine identity associated with globalization that became hegemonic through the Cochabamba water wars was anything but essentialist. The category 'transnational indigenous man' was opened up by a platform that argued for the protection of uses and customs. This platform broke down rural/urban dichotomies, allowed urban Bolivians to claim an indigenous heritage while at the same time giving the alliance of indigenous movements, unions, professionals, women's groups and irrigators an embodied (indigenous) voice that was recognizable in the global arena. It is not only global anti-capitalist and environmental pressure groups that recognize indigenous bodies. The success of donor-funded, socially inclusive neo-liberal development strategies is also monitored by the participation of indigenous leaders in consultation meetings and strategy design (Davis, 2002). The indigenous subject is therefore central to, and powerful in, both donor development with identity paradigms and anti-capitalist understandings of participative, appropriate development.

The masculine subjectivity associated with globalization that successfully became hegemonic through the Cochabamba water wars did so by re-working the link usually made between vulnerability and victimhood in representations of Southern masculinities at a range of scales. The 'unreconstructed gringos' had to go home and Cochabamba and its (hybrid indigenous) heroes became the darlings of the global anti-capitalist movement.

Conclusion

In this paper I have argued that contemporary struggles over establishing development orthodoxy reflect different masculinities competing in the context of rapid globalization. I have indicated that analyzing the use of gendered language illuminates how specific versions of 'modern' development and gendered development subjectivities become pervasive and sometimes hegemonic. I have attempted to illustrate how, in the case of development paradigms and water, actor identities and globalization are at times mutually constitutive of each other. Such a focus on agency is important in studying how development orthodoxy becomes established, because it shows how hegemonic understandings of globalization and the masculine subjectivities they embody can become contested and constructed in the South.

In the current era, globalization is a defining process for development; particularly with regard to its influence on disseminating and reconfiguring neo-liberalism (Laurie and Marvin, 1999). It is not, however, the only global moment that has influenced development trajectories. Successive waves of European, and more recently North American, imperialism and colonialism have long standing global legacies. It is therefore important to recognize the continuities and discontinuities with previous gender regimes in examining the ways in which gendered subjectivities come to embody particular understandings of globalization. In calling for further explorations of the relationship between masculinities and development I am therefore indebted to historical approaches that emphasize the need to understand the gender subjectivities associated with development in relation to changing colonial discourses. In contrast to work on competing masculinities (Connell, 1995; Hooper, 2000a), I have argued that in countries of the South the social epistemology of any given era is seldom consolidated. Development projects and modernizing discourses are incomplete, consequently, the postcolonial context means gender regimes are greatly informed by, yet not frozen in, colonial and neo-colonial power relations.

The gender identities displayed during the Cochabamba water privatization debates are a tale of marginalized masculine subjectivities becoming heroic. By the year 2000 the scene for the competition between hegemonic subjectivities had been scaled up as the heroic masculinities of the Cochabamba water wars became constituted and played out in a global arena. The Cochabamba water wars have become emblematic of Southern, local expressions of the world-wide anti-globalization movements that have recently come to characterize development politics. Not only did the wars succeed in ousting an international water company and changing water privatization laws to recognize cultural water uses and customs but also the leaders of the movement became prominent figures in global anti-capitalist rallies.

In the longer term, on the one hand the Cochabamba experience is inspiring anti-privatization movements in and beyond the Latin American water sector. On the other, the water wars have prompted, one of the most powerful utilities companies in the world (Bechtel, a major partner in Aguas de Tunari), to sue the Bolivian government for breaking their contract. Such issues of global governance are a further illustration of the scaling up of debates over private and public sector investments in development; a transnational private company is seeking to police the ultimate public sector institution, the government of a sovereign State. It remains to be seen who will become the heroes of this struggle. How successful will the diverse gendered actors that emerged through the Bolivia water debates be in defending their specific interest group's definition of modern development, locally, globally and transnationally?

Bibliography

Bakker, K. 2001. 'Paying for water: water charging equity in England and Wales' *Transactions of the Institute of British Geographers* 26(2), 143–164.

Calla, P. 1996. 'Experiencing Revolution in Nicaragua: Gendered Politics in the Negotiations between Nixtayolero Theatre Collective and the Sandinista State'. PhD dissertation Arizona University.

Calla, P. and Y. G. Rojas. 1998. 'Producir, Dar y Proteger: Crisis del Estado Padre Boliviano'. Paper presented at the conference on the Figure of the Father, Asociación del Campo Freudiano de Bolivia, Cochabamba, Bolivia.

Connell, R. W. 1995. *Masculinities.* Berkeley: University of California Press

Cornwall, A. and S. White (eds). 2000. 'Men masculinities and development: politics, policies and practice', special issue *IDS Bulletin* 31(2).

Crespo, C. 2000. 'Continuidad y Ruptura: la Guerra del Agua y los nuevos Movimientos sociales en Bolivia' *Revista del Observatorio Social de América Latina*, No 2, Buenos Aires: CLACSO.

Crespo, C. 2003. 'Water privatisation policies and conflict in Bolivia: the water war in Cochabamba (1999–2000)'. PhD dissertation, Oxford Brookes University.

Davis, S. 2002. 'Indigenous peoples, poverty and participatory development: the experience of the World Bank in Latin America', in R. Seider (ed) *Pluri-Cultural and Multi-Ethnic'-Implications for State and Society in Mesoamerica and the Andes*, pp 227–251. Basingstoke: Palgrave.

De la Cadena, M. 2000. *Indigenous Mestizos: the Politics of Race and Culture in Cuzco, Peru, 1919–1991.* Notre Dame: Duke University Press.

Elson, D. (ed) 1995. *Male Bias in the Development Process.* Manchester: Manchester University Press.

Gill, L. 2000. *Teetering on the Rim. Global Restructuring, Daily Life, and the Armed Retreat of the Bolivia State.* New York: Columbia University Press.

Hall, D. 1999. 'The Water Multinationals', PSIRU Occasional paper. University of Greenwich: Public Services International Research Unit.

Hall, D. 2000. 'Water partnerships – public-public partnerships and 'twinning' in water and sanitation', PSIRU Occasional paper. University of Greenwich: Public Services International Research Unit.

Hooper, C. 2000a. 'Masculinities in transition the case of globalisation', in M. Marchand and A. Sisson Runyan (eds) *Gender and Global Restructuring. Sightings, Sites and Resistances,* pp. 59–73. London: Routledge.

Hooper, C. 2000b. 'Dismenbodiment, embodiment and the construction of hegemonic masculinity', in G. Youngs (ed.) *Political Economy, Power and the Body,* pp 31–51. Macmillan Press.

Jackson, C. (ed.) 2000. 'Special issue: 'Men at work' – labour, masculinities, development', *The European Journal of Development Studies* 12(2).

Jolly, R. 1991. 'Adjustment with a hman face: a UNICEF record and perspective on the 1980s', *World Development* 19, (12): 1807–1821.

Kohl, B. 2002. 'Stabilizing neoliberalism in Bolivia: Popular participation and privatization', *Political Geography* 21, (4): 449–472.

Komvives, K. 1999. *Designing Pro-Poor Water and Sewer Concessions: Early Lessons from Bolivia,* Washington: World Bank Private Participation in Infrastructure, Private Sector Development Division.

Laserna, R. 2000. 'Cochabamba: la Guerra contra el Agua', *Observatorio Social de America Latina, CLACSO,* 2: 15–20.

Laurie, N. 1999. 'More than the blood of earth mothers', *Gender Place and Culture* 6(4): 393–400.

Laurie, N., R. Andolina, and S. Radcliffe. 2003. 'Indigenous professionalization: transnational social reproduction in the Andes', *Antipode* 35, (3):464–491

Laurie, N. and C. Crespo 2003. "Pro-poor' water privatization: ideology confounded in Bolivia?', *id21 Research Highlights:* 26 November: 1–3

Laurie, N. with P. Calla. In press. 'Development, political theory and postcolonialism' in L. Peake, L. Staeheli and E. Koffman (eds) *Feminist Political Geographies.* London: Routledge.

Laurie, N. and S. Marvin. 1999. 'Globalisation, neo-liberalism and negotiated development in the Andes: Bolivian water and the Misicuni dream', *Environment and Planning A* 31: 1401–1415.

Laurie, N., S. Radcliffe and R. Andolina. 2002. The new excluded 'indigenous'?: The implications of multi-ethnic policies for water reform in Bolivia', in R. Seider (ed.) *Pluri-Cultural and Multi-Ethnic'-Implications for State and Society in Mesoamerica and the Andes,* pp. 252–276. Bastingstoke: Palgrave.

Nickson, A. 2001. 'Tapping the market – can private enterprise supply water to the poor?', *id21 Insights* 37, 1–4.

Nickson, A. and C. Vargas. 2002. The Limitations of Water Regulation: the Failure of the Cochabamba Concession in Bolivia, *Bulletin of Latin American Research* 21(1): 99–120.

Radcliffe, S. *et al.* Forthcoming. Gender, transnationalism and cultures of development. In Andolina, R., N. Laurie and S. Radcliffe *Multi-ethnic transnationalism. Indigenous re-development in the Andes.* Notre Dame: Duke University press.

Rathgeber, E. 1990. 'WID, WAD, GAD: Trends in research and practice'. *The Journal of Developing Area Studies* 24 (1990): 489–502.

Shultz, J. 2002. 'Bringing it all back home', *New Internationalist* 342: 34–35.

Silva, P. 1998. 'Neo-liberalism, democratization and the rise of technocrats', in. M. Vellinga (ed.) *The Changing Role of the State in Latin America,* pp. 75–92. Boulder, Colorado: Westview Press.

Sweetman, C. (ed.) 1997. Special issue on masculinities *Gender and Devlopment* 5(2).

Tinker, I. (ed.). 1990. *Persistent Inequalities: Women and World Development.* New York: Oxford University Press.

Vargas, H. and T. Kruse. 2000. 'Las victorias de Abril: una historia que aún no concluye', *Observatorio Social de America Latina, CLACSO* 2: 7–14.

World Commission for Dams. 2000. *Dams and Development a New Framework for Decision Making.* World Bank November 17th 2000. www.dams.org

Youngs, G. (ed.). 2000. *Political Economy, Power and the Body.* Basingstoke: Macmillan Press.

Managing Scarcity of Water: Notes about Political Mobilisations in Poor Neighbourhoods of El Alto, Bolivia

Franck Poupeau

> «We say an activity is economic when it enables us to obtain the utilitarian benefits we seek, or to estimate the extant possibilities of making said benefits available. [...] Were we to rely on historical experience, we would evidence the fact that all economies are and must be sustained by force [...], however, we will not use the term «economic action» to speak about this use of force, which is nothing more than a means at the service of economic action. Another essential fact: economic action is always conditioned by the scarcity of means and is dependant on them for direction ...»
> (Max Weber, *Histoire économique. Esquisse d'une histoire universelle de l'économie et de la société*, Paris, Gallimard, 1991, p.7–8.)

Introduction

Since the 1980s, more and more attention has been focused on problems posed by water management in urban areas, particularly in the outskirts of the big cities of the South.[46] The need to balance available resources has created growing concern over unequal access to water in the large metropoli of Asia, Africa and South America, where uncontrolled development has become an important matter for both international institutions and researchers. Geographical and economic research on this issue has been carried out especially in Africa, but also in India, the Caribbean and South America. These studies have stressed issues concerning the most marginalised populations and the effects they have in terms of hygiene, marketing and access to water.[47] In contrast to what is called *the tragedy of the commons*,[48] these studies highlight the notion that

---

46. Guy Meublat, "La rénovation des politiques de l'eau dans les pays du Sud", *Revue Tiers Monde*, t.XLII, n°166, 2001, p. 249-258.

water shortage is not an inexorable process tied to a disproportionate increase in population relative to limited natural resources, but the result of policies that aim to produce shortage, i.e. that make water an economic good that can be bought and sold in a natural resource market justified by scarcity. In cities where market relations develop under the prevailing form of social and economic exchange, the flow of water joins the flow of capital, money and social power, and offers a different outlook on the development of a city and its organisation. As Erik Swingledow has written: «to control water is to control the city.[49]» This paper has no intention of going as far as Wittfogel's thesis on the Hydraulic State, which has been widely discussed and criticised by historians and anthropologists over the last thirty years;[50] rather, it is a reflection about water, its management control, uses and representations as part of an anthropology of water for developing cities.

With this in mind, the city of El Alto, on the periphery of Bolivia's capital La Paz, provides an excellent example. The scarcity of water, affecting the most underprivileged districts, seems to be associated with the harshness of the geographical conditions that exist at more than 4000 metres above sea level.[51] Another interesting feature of El Alto is the demographic growth that has occurred since the 1960s, with an acceleration in the 1980s, when liberal policies for structural adjustment[52] drove impoverished rural migrants to settle in low-income neighbourhoods. In the 1990s, these policies have led to the privatisation of natural resources, gas and water among them. In 1997, under the impetus of the World Bank, the municipal company SAMAPA (*Servicio Municipal de Agua y Alcantarillado*, or Municipal Service for Running Water and Sewer Systems) was replaced by the *Aguas del Illimani* (Illimani Waters) consortium, of which the French *Suez-Lyonnaise des Eaux* company holds 51% of the shares. At the time, the cities of La Paz and El Alto had 95% and 65% coverage for running water, and 80% and 25% for sewerage. The contract compelled Aguas del Illimani to build 71,752 free connections in the geographical area defined by the concession, to invest USD 80 million in 5 years, and to reimburse SAMAPA's USD 51 –million dollar debt to international agencies.[53] Since no municipal authority was consulted during the privatisa-

---

47. For a review of these studies, see: Sylvy Jaglin, "L'eau potable dans les villes en développement. Les modèles marchands face à la pauvreté", *Revue Tiers Monde*, t. XLII, no 166, 2001, p. 275-303; Graciela Schneier & Bernard de Gouvello (eds), *Eaux et réseaux. Les défis de la mondialisation*, Paris, IHEAL/CREDAL, 2003.
48. Elinor Ostrom, *Governing the Commons. The Evolution of Institutions for Collective Action*, New York, Cambridge University Press, 1990; Elinor Ostrom et al., *Protecting the Commons. A Framework for Resource Management in the Americas*, Washington DC, Insland Press, 2001. For a criticism of this literature, see Michael Goldman, "'Customs in common': the epistemic world of the commons scholars", *Theory and Society*, 26, 1997, p.1-37.
49. Erik Swyngedow, *Social Power and the Urbanization of Water. Flows of Power*, Oxford, Oxford University Press, 2001.
50. For this topic, see the dossier "Politiques et contrôle de l'eau dans le Moyen-Orient ancien", *Annales. Histoire, sciences sociales*, Year 57, 3, May-June, 2002.
51. For an analysis of the conditions to set up a private company, see Christine Komives & Penelope Brook Cohen, *Expanding Water and Sanitation Services to Low-Income Households: The Case of La Paz-El Alto Concession*, Public Policy for the Private Sector, nota n° 178, 1998.
52. See Benjamin Khol, "Privatization Bolivian Style: a Cautionary Tale", *International Journal of Urban and Regional Research*, vol.28 (4), 2004, p.893-908.

tion, numerous local protests took place, especially in El Alto. For example, in the winter of 2004, Fejuve (*Federación de Juntas Vecinales* or the Association of District Committees), mobilised protest against *Aguas del Illimani*. FEJUVE accused the company of failing to meet contract demands pertaining to equipment, and of an excessive increase in installation and consumer prices that rendered access to water services inaccessible to the poorest populations.

These protests were part of the protest cycle that began in Bolivia by the «water war» in Cochabamba.[54] After studying two of the most deprived popular peripheral neighbourhoods of El Alto[55], marked by a lack of water services and by economic hardship, we will present in this paper a critical analysis of the protests that were supposedly spontaneously generated by extreme poverty in these urban areas. By looking at individual and collective ways of adapting to water shortage, we will see to what extent the management of scarcity is inscribed in political processes that are linked to different forms of community organisation.

El Alto: historical and social geography

Towering over the city of La Paz, the «*Aymara city*»[56] of El Alto extends over many square kilometres of the Bolivian *altiplano* (high plateau). A mere rural periphery of the capital in the 1950s, El Alto had become by 2000 the country's fourth largest city with more than 700,000 inhabitants. By the end of the 1980s, the mayor still referred to El Alto as «an urban centre with a rural mentality».[57] El Alto continues to receive migrants from the countryside, who have been driven off their lands by a combination of demographic growth and a policy of parcelling that has reduced the land available to them. Most of the *Aymara* or *Quechua* indigenous people come from the department of La Paz, and especially from the Titicaca Lake area, the historical cradle of the Aymara nationalist movement.

At the beginning of the 20th century, El Alto was still a rural area where community-owned parcels of land and large *haciendas* coexisted on the *altiplano* that lies west of La Paz. From 1910 to the 1950s, some companies (i.e. transportation companies) started to set up business there, in particular along the *Ceja*, the boundary between La Paz and its periphery. By the time of the 1952 National Revolution, the first districts of

---

53. Among them the World Bank, which in 2000 became an 8% shareholder in the consortium thanks to a USD 16 –million dollar loan from its subsidiary, the International Finance Corporation.
54. Franck Poupeau, "La guerre de l'eau", *Agone*, n°26-27, 2002, p.133-140; Andrew Nickson & Claudia Vargas, «The limitations of water regulation: the failure of the Cochabamba concession in Bolivia», *Bulletin of Latin American Research*, vol.21 (1), 2002, p.99-120.
55. For more details about mobilizations in El Alto, see Sian Lazar, «El Alto, Cuidad Rebelde: Organization Bases for Revolt», *Bulletin of Latin American Research*, Vol. 25, No. 2, pp. 183–199, 2006.
56. Álvaro García Linera, "La organización vecinal en El Alto. La Federación de Juntas Vecinales de El Alto" [District Organization in El Alto. The Association of District Committees, *in* Álvaro García Linera (dir.), *Sociología de los movimientos sociales en Bolivia. Estructuras de movilización, repertorios culturales y acción política* [Sociology of Social Movements in Bolivia. Mobilization structures, Cultural Repertoires and Political Action], La Paz, Diakonia-Oxfam, 2005, p.590.
57. Godofredo Sandoval y Fernanda Sostres, *La ciudad prometida* [The Promised City], La Paz, ILDIS, 1989.

El Alto had already been created, among them Villa Dolores (in the south), the 16 de Julio area (the city's biggest market site), and Alto Lima (in the north, overlooking La Paz). Expansion has continued ever since, with a peak during 1975–1985, when workers from the mining centres joined rural migration.[58] The population grew from 11,000 people in 1950 to 30,000 in 1960, and exceeded 350,000 by the mid-1980s.[59] New areas were gradually populated and defined,[60] extending eastward into the Murillo province, while the old neighbourhoods became denser, especially Alto Lima and the southern part. Transportation routes were established between the different districts and they began to transform the rural character of the town into a peripheral suburb of La Paz. By the end of the 1950s the Alto Lima and Villa Dolores districts were provided with running water and electricity.[61] Continuous urban sprawl, however, made it difficult for the newly arrived to have sufficient access to these services. The Alto Lima area continued to develop westward, towards Río Seco and Huayna Potosí, reaching higher sites (4200 metres) towards the north, in the direction of the Andes Mountain Range and along the gap overlooking La Paz.

It was not until 1988 that El Alto acquired autonomous administrative status in relation to La Paz. This new status resulted from the pressure exerted by the first neighbourhood organisations[62] determined to obtain access to collective infrastructure (water evacuation systems, schools, etc.), that the La Paz municipality deemed unnecessary for an area it still regarded as too rural. Since then, three distinct areas have developed in El Alto: the relatively industrialised southern area, with a population that can be defined as mostly «lower middle class» (employees, medium-level executives, arrivals from other departments); the central area, mostly commercial and dedicated to craft industries, with a bi-weekly central market; and the northern area, which has a concentration of rural migrants from the provinces of La Paz and Los Andes, and an emerging «*Aymara* middle class» linked to craft industries, trade and transportation.[63] This socio-economic differentiation shows that the northern area (where both the Alto Lima and Huayna Potosí districts are located) to be the area that is the least economically endowed in terms of infrastructure, industrialisation and quality of life. The geographical expansion of El Alto, which is pushing these districts' borders even farther towards the Andes Mountain Range, has not brought administrative concern for those who live in these distant neighbourhoods and who do not have titles for the land they occupy.[64] At first sight, this institutional vacuum seems to be part of a more general insufficiency that affects the entire set of livelihood conditions of the inhabit-

---

58. UNITAS (Popular Urban Sector), *El Alto desde El Alto* [El Alto from El Alto], UNITAS-Bolivia, 1988.
59. Estimations of the National Statistics Institute (or Instituto Nacional de Estadísticas (INE)).
60. like Río Seco or Villa Ingenio
61. G. Sandoval & F. Sostres, *op.cit.*, p.22.
62. As a result of the efforts of the «Central Council of Neighbours», founded in 1957, and the Independent Unity and Renovation Front of El Alto (*Frente de Unidad y Renovación Independiente de El Alto* (FURIA)), a specific zone was created in 1985 within the province centring on El Alto, and this zone was later given the status of city by the National Congress in 1988.
63. Jorge Castillo, *Situación del Alto Norte* [Situation of the Northern El Alto], La Paz, BIRD, 1983; Raúl Bascón et al., *Mejoramiento del empleo urbano y las condiciones de vida en El Alto de La Paz* [Improvement of urban employment and life conditions in El Alto of La Paz], La Paz, USAID-Bolivia, 1988.
64. Also the reason why they have not been truly incorporated into the district committee networks grouped in Fejuve.

ants of these districts. However, it is crucial to break away from this impression in order to gain a more sociological insight into how social life is organised here (see Box 1: «Phenomenology of ethnocentric perception").

> **(1) Phenomenology of ethnocentric perception**
>
> In describing the research sites in El Alto chosen for this study, it is easy to fall prey to an ethnocentric view that goes all the more unrecognised because of the stark living conditions of the residents. El Alto's geographical situation only stresses the difficulties of daily life there: at more then 4000 metres altitude, cold becomes more intense when the sun sets or is hidden by clouds (as the local saying goes, this sun does not warm you, it burns you). Throughout the year, wind storms sweep over the mostly unpaved wide avenues, causing whirlwinds of garbage and plastic bags that fall haphazardly on the streets. The districts I have studied, Alto Lima and Huayna Potosí, lie on the outskirts of the city, in the northern part of El Alto that extends towards the Andes Mountain Range. This city's border districts are constantly stretched by the uninterrupted arrival of rural migrants – contrasting with the incessant erosion of households in neighbouring rural areas. They are crossed by rectilinear streets or avenues, with their long axes pointing towards the surrounding mountains.[65] These roads intersect with perpendicular streets or avenues (also mostly unpaved), and in these crossroads one might find a flock of sheep or a herd of pigs tied to posts, eating rubbish. Few cars, if any, pass by: only white trucks that can carry a dozen people, or green Dodge buses that resemble a bus of the 1950s, puffing out black fumes and a strong smell of gas. It is rare to pass somebody in the street: the only pedestrians are *cholitas*,[66] with long pleated skirts and a bowler hat firmly set on their head, sitting where they are sheltered from the wind, watching over the few sheep or pigs they own; or, at midday, students in uniform leaving the neighbourhood school.
>
> These aspects of the border districts in the northern area give the impression that one is in a city that is not really a city, a place where everything appears to denote absence: absence of public facilities, of main traffic routes, of drainage systems and sources of water supply, which, in the countryside, serve as a site for social relations, or at least as spatial and temporal reference points in the town's life. In these neighbourhoods, a passer-by's view fails to discover any trace of collective organisation. At the turn of a corner, one may find a Prosalud building, run by an NGO established in all these districts to compensate for the lack of a public hospital. Few people, however, use these facilities because their services are considered to be too expensive. Nor do the local people go to the «*baños públicos*» (public restrooms), which are collective hexagon-shaped restrooms recently installed with co-financing from the United Nations and the French Cooperation.

---

65. Thérèse Bouysse-Cassagne, "*Urco* and *Urma*: Aymara concepts of space", in John V. Murra, Nathan Waechtel & Jacques Revel, *Anthropologies History of Andean Polities*, Cambridge, Cambridge University Press, 1986.
66. The term *cholita* is used for *cholo* women who work mainly as street vendors. During the colonial period, the term *cholo* was applied to descendants of second generation mixed-race people. In the 20th century, the meaning of the term broadened to include low-income urban inhabitants. Nowadays in Bolivia, the term "white" refers in particular to a favoured socio-economic status, whereas *cholo* is used for bilingual *mestizos* (racial mixtures of indigenous and white people, or "purely indigenous" people) who have advanced on the socio-economic scale and have partially adopted cultural features of the "white" people. The term *cholita*, which is the diminutive of *chola*, is considered to be paternalistic. If the Bolivian population is mostly of Amerindian indigenous origin (approximately 60%), 30% are *mestizos* (*mestizos* and *cholos*) and approximately 10% are "white", mainly of Spanish descent.

It is tempting to be carried away by these impressions of absence. Sparsely placed Coca Cola signs are the only «public» presence; on some electric posts, a dummy hangs with a sign warning thieves that they will suffer the same fate if they are caught stealing. On the kerbs of sidewalks, along dry gutters, behind a mound of earth that obstructs the road, masses of accumulated waste attract domestic pigs, dogs, and sometimes small children, who dig and splash about seeking to play or, as in many so-called «developing» countries, something to eat. On some walls one can read «*Garbage kills*». To this apparent institutional and infrastructural emptiness, one might add the trouble of finding people who live in these areas. There are few passers-by in the streets, except for those who are going to one of the few small grocery stores. Residents tend to work far from home and usually stay in their place of work for several days. Instead of an alignment of houses with gardens, small brick or «*adobe*» (mud brick) walls surround narrow gardens and patios, and enclose a one or two-storey main room. These structures give these «residential» neighbourhoods an even more hermetic character, closed to visitors.

The «utilitarian» politicisation of district residents

Most residents of El Alto's northern districts are of rural origin but are not «uprooted» peasants, in the sense used in colonial contexts.[67] They left their homes when they were 14 or 15 years old, i.e. at the age when indigenous families, *Aymara* and *Quechua*, customarily stop supporting their children because they are old enough to work. In both of the districts where interviews were conducted, only a small minority of the residents had lived in El Alto all their lives; others had lived in several houses before settling in these peripheral districts, where the price of land made it possible for them to build a simple house.

Their arrival in El Alto is linked both to the transformation of the Bolivian economy – in particular to the structural adjustment policies that reinforced the rural world's impoverishment – and to the interwoven relations between rural life and life on the periphery of developing metropolis in countries of the South. Just like the direction of the streets, which systematically open to the surrounding mountains, the houses express their dwellers' rural origin. The streets point to surrounding mountains, understood to be the incarnations of the *Pachamama* (or Mother –Earth), which gave birth to the world in Andean mythologies.[68] The houses are oriented towards sunset or sunrise, depending on their location on this or that side of the unpaved streets, thus expressing an adherence to practical rules that have developed in original communities.[69] The internal organisation of the habitat shows constraints of overcrowding and lack of privacy: families living in one room, with juxtaposed beds, little or no other furniture, and a gas stove, around which clothes are spread to dry,.

As for collective life in El Alto, there are «neighbours in charge» who have been chosen to organise Sunday meetings, which is common in rural communities. These neighbours also represent the recognised ties with the district committees grouped in

---

67. Paul Silverstein, «On rooting and uprooting. Kabyle habitus, domesticity and structural nostalgia», *Ethnography –Special Issue: Pierre Bourdieu in the Field*, 5 (4), 2004, p.553-578.
68. For the Pachamama, see Xavier Albó, «Culturas y cosmovisión andina» [Cultures and Andean cosmovision], *Suhupihui*, 41, 1987, p. 9-28.
69. Xavier Albo et al., *Chuquiyawu: la cara aymara de La Paz* [Chuquiyawu: the Aymara FACE of La Paz], La Paz, Cipca, 1983.

Fejuve[70], for whom they transmit calls for action. Even in the case of District 4 of Alto Lima, in which Fejuve is not present because it does not operate in districts where residents lack property titles certified by city hall, somebody is made responsible for the neighbourhood, i.e. someone is selected to organise public meetings and to ensure that collective decisions are upheld by the appropriate authorities.

At the beginning, these community organisation forms can be an obstacle for any study. First, because it is hard to establish contacts and arrange individual interviews. Some neighbourhood representatives refuse to talk and need to be convinced of the valid reasons for the study; they must be reassured that it will not be used as a means by the water company (whose main shareholder is French) to control what they think. Men excuse themselves with unfinished work, and rarely show up for interviews that were scheduled beforehand. Women, when alone, refuse to talk with a stranger: «*It is scary*», as a Huayna Potosí resident said. Some interviews were only possible in groups, when several women neighbours had already gathered. The interviews would not have been possible without the mediation of a taxi driver, Paulino, who lives in the districts studied. He was in charge of knocking on the doors and explaining the reasons for the interview: «*to help us*». Contacts were thus established through a form of participative interviewing,[71] during which people explicitly and repeatedly expressed demands to «do something» for the neighbours, «to help us get water». Understanding their complaint that «*they ignore us, the politicians*» was an important condition for establishing any kind of rapport. In order to establish a long-lasting relationship with the local people, the researcher had to manifest a real interest in the local situation and quickly prove capable of «doing something» for the residents. In each new encounter, the researcher was asked if there is any news about the water and if representatives of the Aguas del Illimani Company had been contacted (being a French researcher seemed to be an implicit guarantee that the consortium built around the Lyonnaise des Eaux subsidiary would indeed grant access).

The rapport that was developed through interviewing the local people revealed the neighbours' specific relation to politics; i.e. relations that could be qualified as «utilitarian» if the term did not imply a devaluation. It reveals that these people do not protest out of simple conviction or spontaneous anti-capitalism, but rather because they need to provide themselves with a livelihood and a decent existence. However, if one were to believe union members, sociologists or journalists positively disposed towards recent struggles, the entire El Alto area would still be vibrating with the formidable success obtained in October 2003 that led to the resignation of President Gonzalo Sánchez de Lozada and to a referendum on the nationalisation of natural resources.[72]

---

70. Álvaro García Linera, «La organización vecinal en El Alto…» [District Organization in El Alto…], *op.cit.*, p.587-620. The Association of District Committees of El Alto groups together district committees that organise neighbourhood life through weekly meetings, in which residents are the decision makers, and also inform residents on collective actions in which they ought to participate as community members. Although almost all Bolivian towns and cities have district committees, the El Alto association of committees was not formed as a lobbying group until the 1970s; since then it has become a large-scale mobilizing social force that participates in political life at the same level as national unions.
71. John Arundel Barnes, "Problèmes éthiques et politiques. L'enquête en contexte colonial vue par un anthropologue du Rhodes Livingstone Institute", *in* Daniel Cefaï (ed.), *L'enquête de terrain*, Paris, La Découverte, 2004, p. 162-180.

Moreover, it is tempting to recall the image of «indigenous populations struggling» to defend their rights. The *«blockages»* carried out in December 2004 and in January 2005 against Aguas del Illimani, led by Fejuve's district committees, are considered to be good examples of this enchanted vision of an *Aymara* city predisposed to righteous rage. Slogans, such as the one coined by the leaders of the Coordinadora del Agua (Water Coordination) in Cochabamba, *«we have lost our fear»*, or *«El Alto standing, never kneeling»*, which refer to the «Black October» uprising (more than 80 deaths caused by military repression[73]), may be an indication of the pride of a people wanting to reject the strong feeling of self-devaluation they acquired during a colonial history of ethnic segregation, but mostly it is the result of the poverty that permeates their daily lives.

Yet, no matter how social leaders and political analysts may see the rebirth of the *«Aymara* nation», it is important to point out the very uncommon nature of the October 2003 insurrection and to consider the symbolic unity of an insurrection directed against a president who embodied the denial of the Bolivian people's identity. Insurrections, recurrent in Bolivia, have generally not been as widespread and always have relied on pre-existing organisational structures: unions, district committees, even semi-clandestine parties (see Box 2: «Socio-political foundations of Bolivian insurrections»). In this particular case, however, it is important to examine the role that the independent sector (small merchants, store owners, transportation company owners, etc.) played in the protests: as Alvaro García Linera has shown, it was not an undifferentiated mass of «people» who revolted in 2003 but, instead, rather well-structured socio-professional groups, active in clearly-defined sectors of the city.[74] Militant mythology, fed by the violence of widely publicised pictures showing groups of hooded demonstrators with stones and clubs confronting law enforcement troops, obscures a true sociological understanding of the real conditions that led to political commitment in these low-income districts.

---

72. Franck Poupeau, "Sur deux formes de capital international. Les 'élites de la globalisation' en Bolivie", *Actes de la recherche en sciences sociales*, n°151-152, 2004, p.126-133.
73. *«El Alto standing, never kneeling»* was the leading slogan of these protests. A faithful and minute account of the protests, based on interviews with residents and leaders of the struggling districts, is given by Luis Gomez, *El Alto standing*, La Paz, Communa, 2004. See also Franck Poupeau, "Les 'guerres du gaz' en Bolivie. Les enjeux de l'exportation des hydrocarbures", *Problèmes dAmérique latine*, 57/58, 2005, p.199-214.
74. Álvaro García Linera, *op.cit.*

(2) socio-political foundations of bolivian insurrections

Ever since the founding of the Bolivian state, the anti-colonial insurrections of 1781, when the forces of Aymara leaders Túpaj Katari and Bartolina Sisa besieged the city of La Paz, have continued to feed the national imagination.[75] Moreover, *blockages* organised in Bolivia since the late 1990s use the same tactic, which consists in impeding access to the country's capital: in effect, the main barriers are placed in El Alto to cut off access both to the airport and to the road that links the capital with Cochabamba or with the Chilean and Peruvian borders. October 2003 was a culminating point in this «state of siege», in particular because repression by governmental forces continued to kindle tensions and exacerbate the popular insurrection. The various demonstrations organised in the city's downtown, around governmental buildings such as the presidential palace on Plaza Murillo or on Prado Avenue, precipitated the resignation of a president who embodied the white elite's control over the country.[76] For several centuries, these elites have built their fortune by relentlessly selling the country's natural resources to foreign capital, be it Potosí's gold in the 17th century, Oruro's tin – which led to the *rosca*'s (ruling clique's) control throughout the first half of the 20th century – or the privatisation of oil, denounced by Sergio Almaraz, from 1950 to 1960.[77]

While the «gas war» consecrated the re-emergence of an indigenous opposition movement, it also called attention to another aspect of the social movement: the «national-popular» movement, which groups together what Bolivian sociologist René Zavaleta called the «multitude» of forces traditionally opposed to oligarchic elites and their imperialist allies, and that culminated in the 1952 National Revolution.[78] Since then, this movement has been fostering the construction of the Bolivian state, in spite of the risks of military coups d'état. In 1979, the «national-popular» movement put an end to Colonel Alberto Natusch Busch's dictatorship and handed power over to UDP (Unidad Democrática Popular or Popular Democratic Union). The organisation of social forces was then framed by leftist parties and by the Confederación Obrera Boliviana (COB, or Workers National Confederation), which brought together workers, students and progressive members of the urban middle classes and promoted a vision of national progress that privileges mixed-race people, but saw indigenous movements as secondary allies in the social movement.[79] With the emergence of the *cocalero* (*coca* producers) movement in the 1990s, and the resurgence of Aymara nationalism,[80] – through Felipe Quispe's MIP (Movimiento Indígena Pachakuti) – the indigenous movement is again playing a main role, contextualised by the defeat of the country's unionist movement in the face of structural adjustment policies.

---

75. Forrest Hylton, Sinclair Thomson (eds), *Ya es otro tiempo el presente: Cuatro momentos de insurgencia indígena* [The Present Already Is Another Time: Four Moments of Indigenous Insurgency], La Paz, Muela del Diablo, 2003.
76. Franck Poupeau, "Sur deux formes de capital international".
77. Sergio Almaraz, *Petróleo en Bolivia* [Oil in Bolivia], La Paz: La Juventud, 1958.
78. René Zavaleta Mercado, *Lo nacional-popular en Bolivia* [The national-popular in Bolivia], México, Siglo XXI, 1986.
79. Silvia Rivera Cusicanqui, "Aymara Past, Aymara Future", *NACLA Report on the Americas*, Vol. 25, No. 3, Diciembre de 1991, p. 18-23.
80. It is also necessary to remember that the *Aymara* identity, so important in recent struggles, is essentially the result – made more visible by the protests of these last few years – of the anti-colonial struggles that were led by the *altiplano* peasant communities. For a historical perspective, see Sinclair Thomson, *We Alone Will Rule: Native Andean Politics in the Age of Insurgency*, Madison, University of Wisconsin, 2003.

If the interviews that were conducted in the Huayna Potosí district and District 4 of Alto Lima failed to support the image of a city spontaneously mobilised against the transnational consortium Aguas del Illimani, it is undoubtedly because the most politically structured social groups were absent in these districts. Huayna Potosí residents did participate in the protests, but not out of rejection of the foreign consortium that should contractually provision them. When asked about their most important need, water provision was systematically mentioned, as was their need for good service at a minimum price. The main complaint they had with Aguas del Illimani was not that it is the product of a foreign multinational, which has pillaged the population's natural resource in order to resell it with a profit, but rather that the company has not attended to the needs of their neighbourhood properly: «*they dont pay us any attention*». A recurrent theme in the interviews, this complaint, however, is directed at both Aguas del Illimani and political representatives. The participation of these residents in the *blockages* is not so much evidence of a militant anti-colonial struggle and the result of Fejuve-linked district leaders' vigorous exhortations, as it is due to a growing awareness by the residents of their individual needs that they want satisfied. The area president is thus perceived as a coordinator, as an information link between residents and the municipal administration, but in no case is she or he granted political leader status. Seen as a figure of local authority, inherited from traditional rural community practices,[81] residents obey the area president more out of habit, the way a custom might be followed, than out of political awareness. Like the sub-proletarians described by Jànos Lanànyi and Ivàn Szelényi,[82] the inhabitants of these peripheral districts of El Alto marked by precariousness have developed a political awareness that rarely extends beyond the present; yet this preoccupation with meeting immediate needs and searching for basic goods does not express a form of depoliticisation. It reveals that, for social groups who are closest to experiencing the urban sub-proletarian condition, a disposition to revolt cannot be sustained if there are no political structures that can frame it locally.[83] More than an act of spontaneous rage, participation in the *blockages* thus appears to be a concerted action carried out in response to the «*summons*» of district leaders.

Management of scarcity

Collective interviews and individual visits revealed that the uses of water cannot be separated from other aspects of existence. The women in Huayna Potosí have lived there for five years; some had come directly from their *altiplano* towns, others had migrated there when they were younger, along with their family, from another neighbourhood of La Paz. Given the chance, the women occasionally work as maids, but usually

---

81. Esteban Ticona Alejo, *Organización y liderazgo aymara* [Aymara organization and leadership], La Paz, Plural, 2000.
82. Jànos Lanànyi and Ivàn Szelényi, "La formation d'un sous-prolétariat rom. Enquête historique sur la condition des gitans dans un village d'Europe centrale", *Actes de la recherche en sciences sociales*, 160, 2005, p. 60-83.
83. Alicia Gutiérrez, "La reproduction de la pauvreté. Sur les échanges de capital social", *Actes de la recherche en sciences sociales*, 160, 2005, p.84-98.

they work at home and take care of the children. Their husbands frequently leave home to work all week on the other side of town and do not come back every night, as the commuting time would be excessive. For these recent migrants, the fact that they have to pay for water is accepted as a sort of fatality, under the notion that «*everything has to be paid for*», even natural resources. Among adults this does not seem shocking: «*Pachamama was paid for, too*», remembers a former seller of animals, 70 years old, who has lived his entire life between El Alto and his native town. For others, it is because in their neighbourhood water is of a different type. In their hometowns, water springs from «*below*»: it comes from the earth, it is pure. In the city, water comes down from the mountains, it is «*contaminated*» by the Miyuni mine, located at a higher altitude some kilometres away from Alto Lima, or it is dirty because the water distribution networks do not eliminate water from the evacuation networks, waste areas and the river, which is the case of Huayna Potosí. If having to pay for water is not considered an injustice, it is also because Aguas del Illimani has been successful in promoting the idea that the company invests a great amount of money in decontamination: it does not sell a natural resource, but a scarce good that has been transformed.[84]

However, the company's investments are not the most salient feature of its management of the neighbourhood's resources. Several demands addressed to its local offices by district residents received no response other than the suggestion that the residents pay and install sewerage systems by themselves through a cooperative, which would then enable them to buy water from Aguas del Illimani or from other private operators. This shows one of the main features of domination. As in all colonial systems, the colonised local populations are put at its service by appropriating their ways of «living together» and their ways of popular community management as a means to promote the company and its approach to the least favoured populations.[85] One cannot imagine «middle class» housewives of the southern area of La Paz creating evacuation networks themselves or building sidewalks, as we did see in Huayna Potosí. Such is the dual system generated by water privatisation in an urban setting: the wealthiest benefit from public facilities while the poorest must face hardships of scarcity, inciting them to find collective solutions, even, later on, to rely on private operators, as is the case of the Ecuadorian city of Guayaquil.[86]

The situation of Alto Lima is somewhat different from that of Huayna Potosí. All of the families we interviewed in District 4 (*Barrio Solidaridad*) asserted that they did not participate in the protests: in the first place, because of the distance, but also and in particular because of their very strong «*mistrust*» of the political class, including of Fejuve leaders. In effect, the association of district committees has not yet recognised District 4 representatives, because its residents do not have property titles. Besides, the call for a widespread blockage and for the expulsion of Aguas del Illimani seems to have been

---

84. Kristin Komives, «Designing pro-poor water and sewer concessions. Early lessons from Bolivia", *Water Policy*, 3, 2001, p.61-79.
85. On how the colonial city operated, see Catherine Coquery-Vidrovitch, "Villes coloniales et histoire des africains", *Vingtième siècle*, PFNSP, n°20, 1988.
86. E.Swingedow, *op.cit*. These examples show the extent to which the liberal discourse of large national institutions can easily recover the "return to the *ayllu*" myth. For the colonial origins of the notion of "community", see John V. Murra and Nathan Wechtel, "Introduction", *in* John V. Murra, Nathan Wachtel y Jacques Revel, *op.cit.*, p.1-9.

quite remote from the local concerns and needs for all types of equipment, which El Alto Fejuve leaders apparently ignore. «*They are politicians*», say residents on this matter, «*like the others*», suspected of building their strategy for public recognition on the misery of the residents who are worst off, and who are used as arguments against the foreign consortium. Some residents even question the priority Fejuve apparently is giving to a tactic of political positioning over a social policy that would support residents, for whom the private, municipal, international or local nature of the water company is meaningless as long as they have no access to water.

Indeed, water is missing where Fejuve is not well established not so much because of a lack of local members, but rather because in those neighbourhoods collective pressure is not strong enough to mobilise Fejuve to act for the benefit of the neighbourhood. This lack of support only stresses the feeling of dispossession and neglect, experienced as a fatality in households where the wage-earner makes – and not regularly – between 20 and 25 *bolivianos* [approximately 3 €] for a day of work in construction. In the neighbourhood, streets are unsuited for traffic, and the irregularity of terrain in some areas – along with the potholes dug to get earth for walls – makes the circulation of water impossible. Even the most visible institutional initiatives, like the public restrooms installed by the French Cooperation, contribute to this collective neglect: restrooms are out of order or in disuse because no municipal worker looks after them.

Faced with a lack of water, it is mainly individual strategies that are set in motion. In Huayna Potosí, wells are dug in the yards of houses if they are not too contaminated (despite diarrhoea problems in children). In District 4 of Alto Lima, the only available well for 200 families is not collectively maintained and the members of each household use their share of containers and pots to attend to their various needs: cooking, washing clothes and washing themselves. The house is organised according to household uses of water, especially for individual hygiene. Baths are taken on the landing during the sunniest hours of the day. Children are bathed, twice or thrice a week, in tubs of water heated on the gas stove; whereas working adults generally wash themselves on the weekend. In case of penury, when wells dry up, the Huayna Potosí and Alto Lima residents are forced to request water from residents of neighbouring districts, who charge as much as they can. This dependency on neighbours is difficult to live with, in particular since they are suspected of over-charging.[87] As a result, power relations are established with districts that lie two streets away and hinder, in multiple ways, the making of a collective neighbourhood identity.

Concluding thoughts

For all these reasons, one can understand why El Alto northern district residents have not reacted as *Cochabambino* peasants did when they expelled the multinational company that was seeking to privatise water distribution some years ago. The latter, bestowed with a strong cultural identity, which had survived through local participation

---

87. Victoria I. Casabona, "El agua: recurso de poder en un barrio periférico" [Water: Power Resource in a Peripheral District], *in* Victoria Arribas et al. (eds), *Constructores de Otredad. Una introducción a la antropología social y cultural* [Builders of Otherness. An Introduction to Social and Cultural Anthropology], Buenos Aires, Eudeba, 1999, p.193-199.

forms and the arrival of former miners, had inherited decade-old militant traditions. In the still new city of El Alto, rural migrants suffer effects of constant strain, strengthened by the permanent absence of any visible and identifiable «oppressor»: «*we have to pay for water, what else can we do?*» Just like the Algerian peasants studied by Pierre Bourdieu, rural migrants living in El Alto are a potential «force of revolution», but not a «revolutionary force»,[88] because their reactions are essentially «utilitarian» in nature, arising out of necessity. Popular revolts are not progressive or conservative *per se*; they acquire meaning only in a political context that guides or fails to guide them against the oppressor designated by the social forces of the moment.

Within this framework, it is evident that the residents of these poor neighbourhoods are subjected to specific forms of domination. Faced with a penury generated by the external appropriation of a resource as essential as water, resigned to the hardships of their daily lives and having lost trust in their political representatives, the residents have devised individual survival strategies that resort to different forms of self-organisation (encouraged by cooperation institutions) in order to respond to their most pressing needs. As shown by Sylvy Jaglin,[89] the alternatives to the crisis of management modes proposed by multinational companies (and the national and international institutions that support them) rely on «people's participation» to supplant the uniform service model. Three types of approaches are thus possible: collective solutions for dealing with basic urgencies (like «*the collective taps*» or collective distribution points); resorting to the informal sector; and finally, a technical and commercial approach, where financing of international cooperation institutions would compensates for the lack of private investment in areas too dispossessed to generate benefits. In the case of Aguas del Illimani in El Alto, the construction of distribution and evacuation networks by residents is believed to reduce by 30% costs and bills. Here, it is clear that a dual system has been put in place: on the one hand, the private sector's usufruct of networks that have already been established in the city's wealthy districts; on the other, popular and «participatory» solutions in areas that are not profitable for private companies or municipal cooperatives. Theorised in World Bank and UN Development Programme publications, and practised «in the field» by international cooperation agencies (USAID, GTZ, French Cooperation), this reutilisation of collective community participation is putting in place a dual system, and contributing to the creation of a scarcity that not only hurts the poorest sectors of the population, but in addition requires them to «participate» more in finding ways to meet their needs.

---

88. Pierre Bourdieu, "Les sous-prolétaires algériens", *Les Temps modernes*, 199, 1962, p.1030-1051.
89. Sylvy Jaglin, *op.cit.*

Irrigation: When the Solution became a Problem

Pablo Regalsky

Introduction

This article will examine the social and economic consequences of micro irrigation schemes introduced by development institutions associated with the introduction of new technologies in Bolivia's high valleys. Even though a number of critical reviews of macro irrigation projects have been published, little attention has been given to the small irrigation schemes promoted by Non-governmental Organisations (NGOs). The aim of this article is to formulate a series of questions related to the impact of irrigation schemes supported by NGOs for agriculture modernization in Bolivia.

Mega Dams have long been a target for criticism, and there is a considerable literature available about the severe damage on the people and on the national economy produced by these initiatives. The irrationality of large-scale dam projects is exemplified by Hendriks (2001:97): i.e. Project Majes in Peru cost 400.000$ per family, irrigates 15.000 Ha (3000 family plots) and had a total cost of $1.300.000.000. As a result of the rising awareness of the human and environmental costs of mega dam projects the reaction of the international development community has been to turn instead to the support of micro irrigation and water schemes. In contrast to the criticism of mega projects, micro projects for water access and irrigation purposes have gained unanimous acceptance in the environment of development aid. In the Andean region, the World Bank states that «(micro) irrigation provides unique opportunities to alleviate (as an economically viable, socially acceptable and low risk solution) poverty in the Altiplano and High Valleys area, as to promote the development of the Low Valleys» (World Bank 1991:11). This thinking is shared by most development NGOs in the region.

An acute need for improving popular urban access to consumption of water on the one hand, and a forceful disposition to preserve the traditional access rights to water for irrigation and human consumption on the other hand, were highlighted by the massive social mobilization that took place in Cochabamba in the year 2000 (Peredo, Crespo et al. 2004). Given this support for improving local water supplies it may then seem a paradox that this paper argues that the institutionalized introduction of micro irrigation schemes, and particularly their impact on the community's social networks and on young women can be highly problematic.

Boelens and Apollin (CGIAR 2005)[90] highlight that «in the Andes, water plays a fundamental role in the different spheres of human coexistence. In the Andean region irrigation systems and water perform a vital social and cultural function. They are intertwined with the symbolic lives of Andean households, as expressed in the many rites and festivals surrounding irrigation». Furthermore, «(g)iven …its ever greater scarcity, irrigation has always been an element of power and conflict» (Ibid.)

These authors also emphasize that two types of irrigation systems currently exist in the Ecuatorean Andes. On the one hand modern systems were created through agrarian reform processes or through the building of such systems, and on the other hand long standing traditional irrigation systems exist. Zimmerer's (1995) research highlights that evidence for such a long standing system exists in the Tarata river alluvial area, 15 km east of Cochabamba city. This system can be traced back to 3500 years ago, and was in use at about AD 719 as an extensive and integrated system of floodwater and canal irrigation measuring more than 50 km (1995:481). He draws attention to the fact that the current modernization of this ancient scheme for irrigation and fertilization by floodwater brought the disruption of the multiple qualities of the former system[91]. A modernization project meant to make more efficient use of water destroyed a network of channels designed in ancient times to take advantage of the periodical flooding for the fertilization of the peasant fields until now. I agree with World Bank consultants Ruf and Apollin (1998) that «the question of irrigation in the Andean region goes beyond mere civil engineering work and (…) consensus building [for modernization purposes]. While it may be spurred by external agents, to be successful it must be a totally endogenous process». The schemes I have seen introduced and managed by outside institutions have changed the rationale of local water use and provoked the disruption of the local productive and social systems.

The problem

My attention was attracted to this issue at the beginning of the 1980's by the Integrated Agricultural Development Project PDAI[92], funded by the Interamerican Development Bank (BID.) working in the central part of the Carrasco province. A small team of students were doing their dissertation fieldwork there in the valley region of Pocona, 100 km east from the city of Cochabamba. Their research was a source of information for a Quechua quarterly that supported their fieldwork. Part of the work of this team was to conduct a survey in the region of Pocona looking at the introduction of several new agricultural techniques by the PDRI (Integrated Rural Development Project), including new hybrid varieties of maize, the improvement of fertilization formulae, and the widening and amelioration of the irrigation net already in place for many generations at that region. These were changes that were supported by micro-loan access for all the families involved[93]. One characteristic of this institutionalized intervention is the pro-

---

90. Date of access to document on internet.
91. Zimmerer, personal communication.
92. PDAI, for: Programa Desarrollo Agrícola Integrado in Spanish

motion of technical change and a market oriented transformation of the traditional agriculture.

During their research the newspaper reported the sudden appearance of suicides in the region. At least 56 people, predominantly young women from a group of villages with a total population of no more than 13.000 in the year of 1986, took their own life. This situation was corroborated by the work of health authorities and the research of a small psychiatric team (Argandoña et al.: s.f). Their final recommendations highlighted the need for better education to be given to the peasants in the region about pesticide manipulation. What strikes most is that no consideration was given to social causes as to why these suicides were happening at that particular moment, or why especially young – and usually married- women were so vulnerable to what they termed an «epidemic». While the predominant world trend of suicide tends to be urban and male, in this area of Bolivia it has emerged as a rural and female trend in certain periods, just as it has in rural areas of India and China in the last two years[94]. No attempt has been made to link the appearance of the epidemics to the introduction of technical change in community life, how this affected social ties and identities in community's cultural life and specifically the role of young women.

While it is difficult to identify the precise causes for the sudden appearance of female suicides, in what follows we attempt to point at some clues. The data collected in this rural context may help to understand how these communities were affected by technical changes. Through frequent visits by the newspaper team to other sites where similar irrigation schemes were being introduced, a pattern appeared connecting the timing of the processes of institutionalized irrigation implementation and the sudden appearance of suicides. A particular characteristic of the pattern connecting these outbreaks of suicide is that they occurred about two or three years after changes in the agriculture system were set in motion and social and cultural changes begin to take place. It should be noted that the victims were mostly young women who take pesticides during, or little after, a feast in a rural setting. This demonstrates a common pattern with the situation in China and India. A sharp rise in suicide was also been observed in the Punata region in the 90's by the Valles Altos irrigation project (PRIV), a huge interventionary project funded by the German Government Technical Assistance (GTZ) to enlarge and interconnect diverse existing communal irrigation systems in the 80's[95].

As Laurie notes in Chapter 6, specific gendered identities become associated with the success of 'modern' development projects. In the case we are examining, the result of technological modernization appears to have reinforced male predominance while making women more vulnerable in several ways.

---

93. Microloans are managed directly by the Project management, replacing the usual exchange of goods between merchants and peasants by the introduction of money lending.
94. *The Lancet* (vol 363, p 1117) 2004, quoted by New Scientist news service April 2, 2004. A similar vacuous assessment is made in India about the causes for suicide: «lack of education».
95. Dr. Kaschiske, GTZ consultant in charge of Punata's Hospital, oral communication at 1994 CENDA Seminar.

The project is known to have had a direct impact on household economies[96]. Research in the Punata region showed that women shared a disproportionate load of work as a consequence of the social changes resulting from the introduction of the irrigation system technical modernization. (Tuijtelaars et al. 1996)[97]. Women are now expected to have overall responsibility for the plots of land. This new level of responsibility has had a direct impact on the social position of women in that they now have to engage in direct contact with men outside the traditional domestic unit, an experience that in many cases has been ruinous due to local and traditional gender norms. This may contribute to explain why young married women are prone to suicide. Technological changes take their toll on the domestic traditions on the role of women.

The changing nature of local economics that resulted from the introduction of new technologies associated with the extension of irrigation schemes by the PDAI can also be determined from the following data:

Table 1. Benefits and costs of peasant corn production at Pocona using two technical levels

Technical level	Output x hectare	Gross Monetary Income (cash sale: M)	Monetary Costs (C)	Net Monetary Surplus (A)	Finantial Yields A/C x 100 = R
«Traditional»	1.105 kg	66.300	27.500	38.860	141 %
«Improved»	1.975 kg	308.100	247.169	69.931	28 %

Exchange rate (1984) 1US$= 2600$b.

Source: Rico (1985)

The table demonstrates that, as a result of technical assistance and improvements produced by micro-irrigation, the productivity of corn improved by the order of 80 %, while the monetary income multiplied 4.6 times. However, the real impact of that improvement was not so beneficial, as the percentage of surplus A, measured against the costs C which have multiplied by a factor of 9 diminished as shown in column R. The yield column shows that the real benefit in monetary terms diminished in relative terms from 141% to 28%.

Consideration must therefore be made of the fact that although big improvements in harvest productivity are usual in the first couple of years of new technologies, after a few years, the production rate will drop dramatically because of the diminishing

---

96. The impact of modernization on peasant cultural life was predicted -as a desirable goal- by José Quitón (1987), a consultant to GTZ at the time, but later on this goal would be disguised by other consultants (Gandarillas et al. 1992).
97. The average suicide rate for young women aged between 15 to 19 living around Vellore in Tamil Nadu was 148 per 100,000. This compares to just 2.1 suicides per 100,000 in the same group in the UK. (New Scientist 02.04.04). Ramiro Tellez, leader of Via Campesina, asserted during a workshop organized in Cochabamba (22.9.05) that the rise of suicide in India as a result of the peasant agriculture crisis induced by the green revolution technologies combined with new water management schemes resulted in more than one million suicides in the last year.

strength of the hybrid seed, the appearance and spread of new diseases, and the impoverishment of soil conditions as a result of the amount of chemicals applied. Moreover, the household economy becomes increasingly vulnerable to market fluctuations and the amount of product sales because its increasing need to expand inputs and repay debts. Industrial inputs are usually received by the peasants as loans from middlemen before the sowing season, and at a very high interest rate. If the family is not able to repay those loans, they will have to let their plot and water rights to the lender or to another, more lucky, peasant from the same community. The new technologies introduce a high element of risk that jeopardizes not only the household income, but also the very basis of existence of the peasantry i.e. their access to land and water[98]. The former domestic food security strategy is replaced by one of commercial monoculture cropping adding increased market risks to an old climatic uncertainty and to new phytosanitary dangers. The more or less self sufficient «traditional» peasant system where inputs and outputs are part of a more or less balanced energy cycle is replaced by an entropic scheme (Calvo et al. 1994). This entropic situation is at the basis of the Andean agricultural crisis, a crisis that has accelerated since the 1983 draught caused by the effects of El Niño. It is part of a generalized process of crisis in peasants' and mountains' productive systems (Dollfus 1981).

One year after the data from Pocona was collected, another part of the team began a comparative study of nutritional levels in children below 5 years in three communities in the neighbouring Mizque province. All three of these communities had different levels of institutional intervention (high, medium and low). In Vila Vila, a community with a high level of institutional intervention, the access to water for irrigation and human consumption was improved by almost 100%. In the second community, Khurumayu, there was a lower level of institutional intervention and roughly half of the population gained access to irrigation. The third community, Raqaypampa, had almost no institutional intervention. It contrast to the two other valley communities Raqaypampa is located on the high plateau at the head of the watershed were the waters feeding the valley's irrigation systems originate. As this last community has no irrigation at all, it has only one agricultural growth cycle during the rainy season (November-March) only, while the other two may have up to three harvests a year.

Located on a high plateau, no irrigation is available and the access to water sources is extremely limited in Raqaypampa. There are few water springs for human and cattle consumption. The local soils are very poor in nutrients and organic matter and they are very thin and erosion prone. Many parts are covered with rocks and have clay subsoil. Only 20% of the area is agricultural soil and erosion affects half of that area. The rainy season lasts three to four months of the year and most rain falls concentrated in short periods of time. Despite these physical signs of poor natural resources, our table 2 (see above) shows that Raqaypampa has the best performance in terms of children nutritional situation.

The following table shows how the nutritional levels of children in these three communities were affected:

---

98. Debt and dependency as a result of introduction of new varieties and toxic chemicals is associated with peasant losing their lands in India during the green revolution but also with grave ethnic and political disturbances (Shiva 1991).

Table 2: Children nutrition levels at three peasant communities in Mizque province.

Malnutrition level	1986			2003
	Tipa Tipa Irrigated	Khurumayu Dry/irrigated	Raqaypampa Dry farming	Raqaypampa
Low	36%	31%	43%	46%
Severe	28%	15%	8%	4%
Total	64%	46%	51%	50%

Source: Hosse, Richter 1986 in Calvo, Regalsky 1994; and Hosse, Camacho in CENDA 2004.

The data show that irrigated communities located very close to marketplaces like Tipa Tipa paradoxically occupy the worst places in order to assure food security to their children as compared with non-irrigated communities, which are located far away from regional marketplaces.

Physical limitations notwithstanding, we find there is a strong food security strategy in place among Raqaypampa's households. All families share a very homogeneous pattern of settlement and resource management as peasant households and behave as reproductive as well as productive units with very marked self-sufficiency and food security strategies that can be summarized as follows.

Peasant space management strategies reproduce on a reduced scale the Andean model of vertical control of multiple tiers: the labour force is better distributed along the yearly cycle by taking advantage of the uneven growth of the rich combination of different crops, different varieties, distributed on altitudinal basis, but also according to microclimate differentials of sun exposure, rain differential and soil differentials. Risk management, germoplasma diversity, and labour management are key factors for food security.

This extremely complex system requires the development of a particular political organization. The community or sindicato (peasant union) is the political frame for the labour exchange between households: it dictates the norms, the customary law that ensure that system to reproduce in a hostile political and economic environment. A community with a good democratic system of self rule not only sustains the balance of everyday life, but allows the collective bargaining of goods for the whole population with governmental or international agencies.

This kind of social engineering is strongly attached to a stock of local knowledge where the handling of diversified germoplasma is the basic structure, with little or no use of technical hardware, forms the basis for the welfare of the families. The rationale for all decisions is based on the household food security. What makes this strategy feasible is an existing family storage facility constructed with local knowledge and that makes possible to keep food up to two years long.

The National Poverty Map[99] made by the UNDP model indicates that more than 90% of the population in Raqaypampa (year 2002 count was 11.700 people) is under the poverty line. Poverty is either defined by the lack of urban services -by UNDP standards- or by a very low monetary income (World Bank 2000).

Who is poor, and by how much?

External pressure, basically in the form of financial help, was a factor responsible for transforming the productive social system in the case of the two valley communities where we now find a weakened food security system. A market oriented monoculture productive strategy was a favoured trend promoted by the aid institutions.

Social nets in Vila Vila and other valley communities were disrupted and the community as polity was weakened, less than 15% of the population took advantage of the market economy obtaining monetary surpluses, buying trucks and other machinery that put them in an advantage situation (Probioma 1991, Meir 1996). The families' food security was disrupted for the other 85% of families that followed suit with the market strategy arrived late to the marketplace with their products, when prices were already falling.

Traditional social links based on the exchange of labour between neighbouring families and reinforced by ritual kinship gave way to a more rationalistic relationship based on salary. As a dramatic sign of what is happening in the community, a tragic symptom arises: small children were suffering most. It may be not only a food deficit and a change in consumption patterns that causes malnutrition, but a relation to negative social circumstances and affective crisis within the families along with imbalances within the community (Aracena 1994). While a growing share of the local production goes to the market, this has two consequences that affect household food security: on the one hand it creates a growing internal social differentiation, whereby many families lose control over their land and water. On the other hand, the consumption pattern changes while people lose food selfsufficiency because staple now has to be bought. These «material» consequences have an unexpected side: we can now understand children malnutrition as well as the female suicides within changing social and technological environments as expressions of *anomia*. Durkheim (1994) famously showed how this process appeared at times of change when traditional roles were disrupted and the individual's sense of purpose was lost.

There's no need to disguise that Andean agriculture is in general suffering a deep crisis as a result of modernisation. It all began in 1983, when a very severe drought took place throughout the Andean region. This sparked the large-scale arrival of aid in the form of exotic potato seeds, agricultural industrial inputs and micro financing. The long term transformation of peasant agriculture became a top priority of the Bolivian government due to the implementation of structural adjustment and the World Bank policies for the introduction of micro irrigation and micro financing. What those people didn't consider was the real needs and the rationale of the Andean agriculture, and the Andean community life in more general terms (Morlon 1992, Golte 1980).

---

99. INE (2002)

A wrong diagnosis has purposely been made by development agents in order to show that the crisis was caused by the lack of technical improvement, as a case for the failure of new techniques and need to strenghthen the local peasant economy did not fit with the existing international trend (Gray Molina, Muñoz et al. 2001). Another leg of this diagnosis was to portray peasant households as responsible for their own lack of access to markets, and so an improvement in income would come as a result of the opening of new market opportunities. We see that in 100% irrigated regions such as Pocona, that have the best locations and access to market through highways, and whose crops are entirely commercialized, the communities are now deserted by the producers. At the same time, non-irrigated regions like Raqaypampa, are now over-populated as the local peasants don't want to leave their communities. This is a consequence of the social impact of the new technologies and the vertical introduction of irrigation schemes that disarticulates community's life, on top of the economic and financial negative results our data shows.

What really happens when new technologies are introduced?

Table 3: Harvest productivity and income-yields with two technological levels 1986/87.

	Traditional Technology	Improved Technology
Output kg/ha	6486	13 454
Nominal income-yields: (Market Price minus Total Cost) x 100/Total Cost	43.5%	(17.5)%
Monetary return: (Total sales x Monetary costs) x 100/Monetary costs	201%	(50%)
Productivity: outcome as harvest kg/manpower hours	8.38	14.5

Source: 1: CENDA y 2: ARADO-PDAR (1988)

The table highlights a paradox: on one hand there is an increased harvest productivity (output), on the other the financial results (nominal and monetary returns) are negative.

As we can see in tables n° 1 and 3, the improvement in harvest productivity works as a rationale for the introduction of this techniques. The increase in productivity means a surplus can be designated for the market. As a result this improvement will appear as a big leap in the income generated and in labor productivity[100]. What is not so apparent is that this surplus does not necessarily mean an equivalent surplus for the local economy. Indeed, after one or two harvests, the peasant producer will see that he cannot make ends meet. By the time the peasant becomes aware of his situation it will be too late because by then he will be heavily indebted. But the results are not merely economic, the changes at a technical level will also entail the transformation of community life, a huge cultural change.

We find that the introduction of the imported or exotic seeds and the green revolution package with the help of subsidies, and the radical transformation of the peasant's productive system by a disruptive institutionalized introduction of new irrigation technologies may have resulted in the disruption of the social networks that made the community.

This is in strong contrast to highland communities where social networks have been preserved for the benefit of everyone and local knowledge still prevails, notwithstanding their «poverty» conditions, even though migration is growing in the last few years and the worsening situation of the exchange terms also affects their livelihood. Changes do not take the character of a permanent rupture with the «organic structure» (Durkheim 1994) of the community and the balance of the situation is kept under control as shown by table 2 for nutrition values. On the other hand, «poor» communities as Raqaypampa maintain very low migration rates. On the contrary, a high rate of permanent migration is evident nowadays in Pocona and other «modernized» communities.

Conclusion

In this paper I have argued that the implications of small scale irrigation introduction to Andean rural communities through institutionalized projects, along the lines of agricultural modernization, have to be questioned and study made of the complex interactions involved when these projects are used as channels for the introduction of new technologies. These technologies become a financial burden for the domestic units as evidenced in the case we examined. There is not only radical change in the usual pattern of self sufficiency for the peasant domestic units that now have to deal with a more dependent and vulnerable economic scheme, but this may also promote the transformation of the existing collaborative working relationships within and between families, resulting in the serious disruption of social and personal life. It not only appears to take a heavy toll on women as the appearance of a high rate of suicide shows[101], but more generally demonstrates the failure of the declared purpose of development institutions which promote modernization as a means for the improvement of rural life and of peasant economy.

---

100. Chayanov asserts in 1924: «the household has to take advantage of the market situation and the natural conditions in such a way that it allows the family to keep an internal balance, together with the higher well being possible. This may be achieved introducing into the organic structure of the farm a labor investment such that will promise the highest possible payment per labor unit. « (Chayanov 1981:55)
101. Ramiro Tellez, leader of Via Campesina, asserted during a workshop organized in Cochabamba (22.9.05) that the rise of suicide in India as a result of the peasant agriculture crisis induced by the green revolution technologies combined with new water management schemes resulted in more than one million suicides in the last year.

Bibliography

Aracena, Carolina 1994. *Madres de niños carenciados en el marco afectivo y alimentario en Bolivia*. Estudio preparatorio para PhD en psicología en la Universidad Católica de Lovaina.

Argandoña, Mario; Butrón, Kathia, Vera, Jenny. (sf) *El suicidio entre la población de Pocona*, informe preliminar. s.e.

Boelens, Rutgerd; and Frédéric Apollin. *Andean Irrigation: a Social Construction.* http://www.iwmi.cgiar.org/respages/PGW/andeanbook.htm accessed on 28.2.05.

Calvo, Luz María; Regalsky, Pablo; Espinoza, C. y Hosse, T. 1994. *Raqaypampa: Los complejos caminos de una comunidad andina.* Cenda, Cochabamba.

Calvo, Luz María; P. Regalsky *et al.* 1994. *Raqaypampa. Los complejos caminos de una comunidad andina.* CENDA, Cochabamba.

CENDA (2004) *Informe sobre situación nutrición infantil en Raqaypampa.* (mimeo). Cochabamba.

Chayanov, Alexandr Vasilevich 1981. *Sobre la teoría de los sistemas económicos no capitalistas.* In *Chayanov y la teoría de la economía campesina,* Cuadernos de Pasado y Presente, nº 94, siglo XXI, Mexico.

Dollfus, Olivier 1981. *El reto del Espacio Andino.* IEP, Lima.

Durkheim, Emile 1994. *El Suicidio.* Ed. Coyoacán. México.

Gandarillas, Humberto; Salazar, Luis; Sanchez, Loyda; Sanchez, Luis y De Zutter, Pierre. 1992. *Dios da el agua. ¿Qué hacen los proyectos?. Manejo de Agua y Organización Campesina. Experiencias en el Proyecto de Riego Inter-valles (PRIV-Cochabamba – Bolivia).* Serie el Desarrollo en Cuestión, 4. Proyecto de Riego Inter Valles – PRIV- HISBOL, La Paz

Golte, Jürgen 1980. *La racionalidad de la organización andina.* Instituto de Estudios Peruanos, Lima.

Gray Molina, George; Muñoz, Jorge; Sánchez de Lozada, Diego *et al.* 2001. *Poverty and Exclusion,* Part II, Chapters 4, 5 and 6, in: Crabtree, John and Whitehead, Laurence (eds). *Towards Democratic Viability. The Bolivian Experience.* Palgrave. Oxford.

Hendriks, Jan 2001. Los derechos de agua y el fortalecimiento de organizaciones de usuarios. In Boelens, R. and Hoogendam, P. (eds): *Derechos de Agua y Acción Colectiva.* IEP, Lima. pp 85–111.

INE, Instituto Nacional de Estadística. 2002. *Bolivia: Mapa de la Pobreza 2001.* La Paz.

Meir, Marga. 1996. *Fortalecimiento de las comunidades andinas para un etnodesarrollo.* Tesis para optar al grado de Ingeniería Agronómica, Universidad de Viena.

Morlon, Pierre. 1992. *L'agriculture paysanne dans les Andes Centrales.* INRA, Paris.

Peredo, Carmen; Crespo, Carlos; Fernandez, Omar. 2004. *Los regantes de Cochabamba en la Guerra del Agua.* CESU-UMSS, Cochabamba.

PROBIOMA 1991. *Factores socioeconómicos que inciden en el manejo del medio ambiente en los valles altos.* PDAR, Cochabamba (mimeo).

Quitón, José. 1987. *Estudio socioeconómico del área de influencia del Proyecto Riego Punata.* CIPLADE, GTZ-IBTA, Cochabamba (mimeo).

Rico, Fernando. 1985. *Economía Campesina y Tecnología en la producción de Maíz en Pocona.* Tesis para optar a la licenciatura en Economía. UMSS, Cochabamba.

Ruf, Thierry and Apollin, Frédéric (1994) *Community based water management in irrigated Andean agriculture: From research to diagnosis, from negotiation to renovation of the irrigation system of the town of Urcuqui, Ecuador.* http://srdis.ciesin.columbia.edu/cases/ecuador-002-en.html accessed on 28.02.05.

Shiva, Vandana. 1991. *The Violence of the Green Revolution. Thirld World Agriculture, Ecology and Politics.* Third World Network, Malaysia.

Tuijtelaars, C., M. E. Pozo, R. M. Antezana y R. Saavedra. 1996. *Mujer y riego en Punata. Aspectos de género.* Programa de Enseñanza e Investigación en Riego Andino y de los Valles. Cochabamba, PEIRAV-UMSS-UAW.

World Bank (1991) *Bolivia Agricultural Sector Review.* Report nº 9882-BO, Latin American and the Caribbean Regional Office.

(2001) *World Development Report 2000.* Washington.

Zimmerer, Karl. 1995. The Origins of Andean Irrigation. *Nature,* vol 378, pp 481–483.

Part III

Local Level Water Management and the Progress of Civilizations in the Ancient Near East: A comparative case

Oystein La Bianca

Abstract

The Ancient Near East (ANE) is frequently referred to as the «cradle of civilizations.» In this paper I highlight ways in which local level water management—as opposed to centralized control of water--has played a role in the development of various pristine and secondary civilizations in the region. To this end I begin by offering a brief overview of theoretical issues pertinent to the study of water and civilizations in the ANE. Next I survey the contribution of local level water management to the progress of various civilizations, including those of ancient Mesopotamia, Egypt and the Levant. I conclude by discussing ways in which lessons learned from the past might inform planning for future supply of freshwater in the region.

Introduction

Much of what has been written and said about the history of water and civilization in the Ancient Near East (henceforth ANE) has focused on engineering and organizational achievements related to advances in state-level control and management of fresh water. A well known example is Wittfogel's (1957) hypothesis linking the rise of powerful despotic rulers in Mesopotamia and Egypt to the managerial requirements of canal based irrigation and agriculture. Another is Reifenberg's (1955) effort to connect advances in agriculture in Palestine to state sponsored construction of large scale water distribution projects—such as the miles of aqueducts built by the Romans. No doubt a major reason for this tendency among scholars to focus on instances of centralized control of freshwater in antiquity is the abundance of archival sources available from places where state level control at times was very strong (esp. Egypt and Mesopotamia). This situation is all the more reason to be cautious about the sort of essentialism that renders marginal all other forms of water control than that involving state-level administration.

The point of the present essay is to argue that the progress of various civilizations in the ANE has depended as much, and perhaps even more, on local level control of water as it has on state level control. This argument proceeds from a fundamental tendency with regard to the state-level polities that normally drive the forward thrust of civilizations—namely their tendency to be transient.[102] The long-term progress of civilizations is therefore normally not a linear process, but an undulating journey of ups and downs. It is for this reason that local level practices are so important, for being more resilient and thus less vulnerable to exhaustion and collapse, they have far greater staying-power. They thus provide civilizations with a solid sub stratum on top of which successive dynasties and associated state level projects can rise and fall.

I begin this paper by offering a brief overview of theoretical issues pertaining to the study of water and civilizations in the ANE. Next I survey the contribution of local level water management to the progress of various civilizations, including those of ancient Mesopotamia, Egypt, and the Levant. I conclude by discussing ways in which lessons learned from the past might inform planning for future supply of freshwater in the region.

Theoretical issues

As already indicated, Wittfogel's hydraulic civilization hypothesis--as presented in Oriental Despotism: A comparative Study of Total Power (1957)--remains the single most influential treatise on water and civilization in the ANE. As grand theory it remains without rival. Although dismissed by many as a distortion of the facts on the ground, its great merit is that—because of its scope and parsimony—it initiated and continues to foster cumulative thinking and research about water and civilization in the ANE and beyond (c.f. Hole 1995:2716). As a result we know today that river basin irrigation agriculture need not depend on complex administration (Fernea 1970; Adams 1981). We also know, however, that where such agriculture exists, it is a most convenient and attractive target of elite domination. And once captured and harnessed by an ambitious elite, it offers enormous potential as a means to power, wealth and influence—indeed, to the rise and development of civilizations![103]

Anthropological research on civilizations has emphasized the difference between 'great' and 'little traditions' (Redfield 1955; 1962; Marriott 1955; Bodley 2000). It is a distinction that has great relevance to our task here. A civilization's great traditions are normative principles and behaviors propagated by its literate elites who are the primary custodians of the canonical texts. Its little traditions, on the other hand, are the con-

---

102. For an excellent discussion of the vulnerability of state-level polities, see Robert McC. Adams 1965.

glomerate of vernacular or local knowledge[104] and practices considered normative by the largely non-literate masses not derived from a canonical text.

'Great traditions' are disseminated by means of universalizing agents (Marriot 1955).[105] Such agents include empires, dynasties, and sometimes religious movements. Agents disseminate 'great traditions' by means of projects – concrete undertakings of various kinds that expand the reach of a 'great tradition.' Modalities are transmission vehicles associated with particular projects and links are places along a chain of geographical points linking a particular 'great tradition' with a particular region or site. Whereas little traditions can persist and change without reliance on the process of universalization, great traditions depend on a network of transmission centers in order to persist and change.

For the purposes of this study, we will define great traditions simply as *universalized collective heritage and knowledge*; and little traditions as *localized indigenous heritage and knowledge*. Defined thus, the concepts are sufficiently broad to accommodate research not only on the ideological aspects (literate vs illiterate) of civilizations, but also on their material aspects (for example, water management systems).

Below these distinctions will be used as a basis for analyzing the management of fresh water resources in various ANE civilizations. Specifically our project here is to identify the little traditions upon which specific civilizations were founded and upon which they relied during times of exhaustion and collapse. How certain of these little traditions were turned into elite-controlled great traditions will also be noted.

Elsewhere (LaBianca 2004) I have discussed how Great and Little Traditions cooperate to produce long-term cycles of intensification and abatement in local food systems which, in turn, are reflected in changes over time and space in historical landscapes and in region-wide and local policies and practices for controlling fresh water resources. In this paper I compare the history of freshwater management in three ANE

---

103. Elsewhere (LaBianca 2004) I have defined 'civilization' as the luminous constellation of radiant attitudes, beliefs, behaviors, values, elite cultural traditions, institutions and works of art, artisanry and architecture that emanate from a particular center such as ancient Sumer, Thebes, Athens or Rome. In this definition three terms—luminous, radiant and constellation–have been drawn from astronomy for the sake of facilitating systematic thinking about the role of civilizations throughout the ANE. Civilizations are luminous when they emit «light» that advances the development of human societies and cultures. Such light might be contributions to the development of writing and language or innovations in such varied fields as religion, technology, commerce, science or the arts.

104. Redfield's framework has been famously applied to the study of Middle Eastern society by Gustave von Grunebaum (1955). In *Unity and Variety in Muslim Civilization* he uses it to examine the interaction between *dar al-Islam*, the «genuine» great tradition, and local culture patterns (1955:27-29). Even though this particular application has been widely criticized (Lukens-Bull 1999), the framework continues to be used and adapted by anthropologists as a means to study interactions between elite cultural traditions and the cultural patterns of commoners (Odner 2000; Bodley 2004).

105. According to McKim Marriott (1955), a student of Redfield, a great tradition owes its existence to two processes. The primary process is *universalization*, by which Marriot meant «the carrying forward of the material which is already present in the little traditions in the villages to a body which «universalized» the knowledge into a great tradition… The second process is *parochialization* or the «downward spread» to the villages of the great tradition. Both *universalization* and *parochialization* are characterized by transformations, and there are gaps in communication which the communities fill at their own discretion» (Marriott 1955 as cited in Odner 2000:34).

regions, namely Mesopotamia, Egypt and the Levant as a means to learn more about the respective contributions of Great versus Little Traditions.

Southern Mesopotamia

Other than the less than 200mm of rain that falls each year between October and May — an amount significantly below that needed to carry on sedentary agriculture--the main source of fresh water in Southern Mesopotamia is water from melting snow drained into headwaters in the Central Anatolian Plateau and transported to the Mesopotamian lowland by the Euphrates and Tigris rivers in two parallel channels (Charles 1988: 6). While the Euphrates follows a meandering channel which runs relatively high with respect to the surrounding flood plain, the Tigris has a much deeper channel and follows a much less meandering path, a fact which makes its late spring floods more violent and its waters more difficult to tap for irrigation (Charles 1988: 6). Over the past five thousand years, flood trends for the two rivers have oscillated between long periods of higher than average floods and long periods with lower than average floods (Butzer 1995: 133).

The earliest experiments with irrigation agriculture in Southern Mesopotamia were undertaken already during Late Neolithic times or about 6000 – 5000 B.C. by early farmers at Samarra. These incipient efforts at irrigation took place along tributary streams of the two great rivers where natural contours and small man-made ditches were combined to create primitive canal systems (Saggs 1988: 8). The development of these systems coincide with expansion of cattle breeding and village life as well as with the appearance of a distinctive type of pottery known as Samarran—which is why this whole culture is sometimes referred to as «Samarran culture» (Hansen 1997: 473; Hole 1997: 135).

The first to successfully tap the waters of the main channels of the Tigris and Euphrates for irrigation were the Ubaid people, who lived ca 5000–3500 B.C. in southernmost Mesopotamia (Adams 1981: 52–60). This was no minor achievement given the very real danger of massive flooding by either river just as crops would be ready for harvesting. A key component of their system was timely organization of labour to keep the natural levees along the river banks from leaking (c.f. Gasche 1988:41–43). Another was successful transfer of water from the main river channels to man-made canals for transporting water to adjacent agricultural fields. The Ubaids also were the first to employ canal inspectors to look after the expanding local networks of fortified levees and abutting canals (Saggs 1988:8; Steinkeller 1988:87). Significantly, these achievements were all made by village level farmers—there were no cities or urban-based elites yet in existence.

The first instance of irrigation associated with urban centers occurs during Uruk times, ca. 3500 to 3000 B.C. According to Adams (1981: 60), what is especially notable during this period is the «mass appearance of sedentary cultivators around regionally differentiated hierarchies of urban centers.» In other words, the huge expansion in village-based canal irrigation that occurred during this period appears to have produced a distinctive settlement pattern involving urban centers surrounded by market towns which, in turn, were encircled by clusters of smaller villages. Each of these villages had their own local network of canals on which they depended for irrigation. Significantly this hierarchical rural settlement pattern coincides with the first instances of monumental buildings and use of cylinder seals and writing. This has led many scholars to conclude that some sort centralized administration exerted influence over the affairs of these village farmers during this period (Saggs 1988: 9).

According to Adams (1981: 75), urban dominance of rural hinterlands during Uruk times was by no means linear in the direction of ever increasing centralization of power. Instead his survey data points to unabated and often ruinous competition between various city-states for control over rural hinterlands. A consequence of this situation was that most urban centers tended to be fledgling and transient depending on the success or failure of their competition for dominance over rural hinterlands. By contrast, village settlements tended to be more resilient, more likely to go on existing despite the predation of urban elites. Thus «little traditions» appear already in Uruk times to provide the baseline wherewithal those incipient civilizations needed in order to succeed in establishing themselves in particular localities.

This pattern of on-again off again control of rural hinterlands by urban centers continues throughout the entire history of ancient Southern Mesopotamia. Eventually a «great tradition» establishes itself that has the following features: 1) elite domination of agricultural labour and canals by means of an agro-managerial bureaucracy centered in city-states; 2) application of various social technologies--for example, priestly regulation of the agricultural calendar--as a means to ensure elite control of agricultural production (Eyre 1955); 3) use of cylinder seals as a means to empower officials and delegate authority within an elite-controlled agro-managerial bureaucracy.

The place where this great tradition first became fully established was Ancient Sumer (Kramer 1963; Woolley 1965). Crucial to the progress of this great tradition was the Sumerian language and script—cuneiform—which not only facilitated routine administrative activities of the Mesopotamian city-states, it also served as an important medium for dissemination of sacred temple literature, epic poetry, and royal decrees. Like its Egyptian counter part, the Sumerian Great Tradition shaped the elite cultural traditions of a succession of dynasties and empires in the Mesopotamian heartland and beyond, starting ca 3500 B.C. and ending ca 500 B.C.

Egypt

Apart from its reliance on water from a great river—the Nile—there is relatively little that ancient Egypt otherwise had in common with ancient Mesopotamia. To begin with, rainfall along the Nile Valley is even scarcer than in the Tigris-Euphrates Valley—way below the minimum for rain fed agriculture. Second, thanks to the evening-out effect of numerous tributaries at its source in Ethiopia, the annual flooding cycle of the Nile is less violent and more predictable by the time it reaches Upper Egypt when compared to that of the two great rivers to the north. And third, water for agriculture along the Nile was much less dependent on networks of canals. Instead, during the flooding season water would spill over at low points along the Nile's natural levees thus inundating adjacent flood basins.[106] These basins, in turn, would be submerged in water for about two months during August and September until the river level dropped below the elevation of the basin floor. The clayey make-up of the soils assured that they retained their moisture for months, allowing the traditional farmer to broadcast his seed during October and November and harvest its produce in February and March before the hot winds of spring (Butzer 1997: 249–250). Herodotus (as cited in Bowman 1986:13) summarized the process well: «they merely wait for the river of its own accord to flood their fields; then when the water has receded, each farmer sows his plot, turns the pigs into it to tread in the seed and then waits for the harvest.»

To a much greater extent than in Mesopotamia, irrigation during the dynastic period in Egypt was, therefore, «essentially a local matter» (Baer 1971)—the stuff of little traditions. Not surprisingly there are no pictures showing the irrigation of fields, no accounts of the methods, no administrative records about the construction, maintenance, or operation of irrigation systems…it is taken for granted, just as houses are never shown in tombs from the Old Kingdom» (Baer 1971).[107]

What is known about the beginnings and history of irrigation in Egypt is the result primarily of archaeological and geoarchaeological investigations in the three main parts of the country, namely the Nile Valley, the Fayyum Depression and the Delta. They have revealed that wheat, barley, pulse and flax have been the staple crops of Egyptian agriculture since prehistoric times (Butzer 1976; Wetterstrom and Murry 2001);

According to Butzer (2001), the history of irrigation agriculture in the Nile Valley has proceeded over three stages. The earliest and therefore the longest lasting—as it was begun during prehistoric times and practiced right up till the mid-twentieth century—is called recessional or *eotechnic* agriculture. It requires no manipulation of the water whatsoever—merely planting of seeds, such as cereals and flax, in the moist alluvial soils as the water in natural flood basins recedes following inundation. To this very basic technique a second, somewhat more sophisticated one was added during dynastic times. Called *paleotechnic* or pharonic irrigation, it involved cultivators compensating for «lower-than average floods by cutting sluices into the levees, or attempt to limit the incursion of unusually high floods by reinforcing levees or plugging up breaks in them» (Butzer 2001: 184). The third, and last, is artificial or *neotechnic* irrigation which the construction of irrigation ditches and canals and techniques for mechanically lifting the water, such as the *shaduf*, or sweep (Butzer 2001: 185). Both *paleotechnic* and *neotechnic* are attested already during late Predynastic times, but it was not till the Ptolomies, that *neotechnic* or artificial irrigation really took off. Concludes Butzer (2001: 187) «the transition from eotechnic, recessional agriculture to paleotechnic irrigated farming was incremental and took place primarily at the grass-roots level.» He adds «irrigation was never maintained or regulated by an administrative bureaucracy; instead, it functioned at the local level, beyond the purview of the pharaoh.»

It is thus clear that in Egypt, even more so than in Mesopotamia, irrigation agriculture belonged to sphere of little traditions (Iliffe 1995: 20). To the extent that it became

---

106. According to Butzer (1976) the Nile floodplain was «subdivided into shallow basins, as a result of the intersection of various active and older levees.»

107. This is perhaps a bit overstated. Butzer (2001: 187) writes with regard to pharonic Egypt that «Basin irrigation was the norm and therefore elicited few directives and no explanatory comment. Estate irrigation and commercial crops, representing only a tiny fraction of the arable land, attracted most of the explicit attention.»

enmeshed within the great tradition, it was at the ceremonial level of centralized regulation of the agricultural calendar by religious elite with the pharaoh at the top (Robins 1995: 1811–1812). During flooding season, Pharonic intervention may also have impacted local agriculture through diversion of agricultural labour to build pyramids (Mendelssohn; 1974; Iliffe 1995: 20).

The Levant

The Levant is made up of the fertile highlands of coastal Syria, Lebanon, Israel, Palestine and Jordan (Tubb 1998:13). Along the coast and in the highlands to the west of the Jordan Valley rainfall can exceed 800 mm annually. The central and northern highlands to the east of the Jordan River can receive in excess of 600 mm annually. As one moves eastward and southward beyond the Syrian and Transjordanian highland rainfall tapers off to less than 200mm annually. The western frontier of the Arabian dessert follows a meandering line running north to south through Syria and Jordan. In a normal year rain falls from October to March—in a wet year from September to May and in a dry year from November to February.

Unlike either Mesopotamia or Egypt, much of the Levant is made up of mountainous highlands intersected by wide valleys and steep canyons. This topography interacts in important ways with local rainfall conditions to produce a range of different natural sources of freshwater. To begin with is the varied pattern of rainfall, which in part is attributable to elevation differences in the landscape. Thus the Dead Sea gets very little rain, while the mountainous highlands and their piedmonts receive the most.

Second is the down slope drainage, which presents opportunities for harvesting run-off water by means of terracing, diversion dams, reservoirs and cisterns. Such run-off collection installations are ubiquitous throughout the highland regions of the Levant, and have even been adapted to harvest rainfall in regions receiving minimal rainfall, such as the Negev and Southern Jordan. There is a great description of how this system worked at the beginning of the 20th century, over 100 years ago, in Libbey and Hoskins (1905):

«Two hours north of Hesban, while traversing the line of the old Roman road, we noticed the curious way in which miles of gently sloping lands had been divided into great terraces by lines of black rock built with cement into dikes that ran all over the country. At places, the level terraces resembled great tennis courts. As we neared Hesban and the Hill about the ancient city, these walls or dikes increased in number and in many cases ran like rulers straight up and down the hillsides. When near Hesban itself, we notices that nearly every terrace or slope had a cistern at its lowest corner, and it at once became clear that this was an ancient device for dividing and securing the rainwater which fell on each man's land. On the more rocky slopes the rain was, of course, the only «crop», and each owner guarded his rainfall as carefully as modern ploughmen do their portion of the running streams. Recalling what we had seen in the Ajlun district, and noting the similar diking about Madeba, Diban, and a dozen other sites, the whole system became clear. There is not a tree or a fountain for miles on that Mishar plateau, and it is very plain that the ancient inhabitants depended almost wholly upon cisterns, of which there are thousands in and about the larger ancient sites. As an addition to the cisterns, they also constructed open pools, which caught the rainfall of larger areas than any one individual could control. At Hesban are the remains of a tank one hundred and thirty-nine feet by one hundred and thirty-nine feet, having a depth of at least ten feet. Another and much larger one will be noticed at Madeba.»

Third is seepage of rain water below ground into natural subterranean reservoirs and aquifers. These, in turn, replenish the underground headwaters of natural springs and streams that appear in various locations throughout the landscape and provide fresh water for parts or all of the year for local residents and visitors alike. Such springs and streams are especially plentiful along the wadies and slopes draining into the Jordan valley and the Dead Sea.

Fourth are the *wadies* or dry river beds that during the rainy season transport run-off and flood waters to lowlands below. While most remain dry all year except following heavy rains, a few are so well endowed with springs and small tributary streams that they have water running in them for most or all of the year. Some, such as the Yarmouk, Zerka, and Moujib in Transjordan are rivers that run all year. The degree to which wadies contain moisture all year can be estimated in part from the quantity of oleander and other water loving plants that inhabit their banks.

Fifth is the dew water that condenses naturally on plants and stone surfaces during night time. The greater the variance in temperatures between night-time and daytime--which depends in part on topographic factors--the greater the amount of dew water produced. Throughout the Levant dew water, supplemented at times by water harvest by means of terraces, has been the main source of irrigation for crops produced by «dry farming» methods. Not only cereals, but also vegetables and tree crops can be produced by this means. Often small stones are piled in a circle around trees or small vegetable gardens to increase the amount of irrigation from dew water. This is sometimes called «stone mulching.»

To these largely local-level water management techniques transient state-level projects were added during certain time periods. In particular the Roman Great Tradition is notable for its heavy emphasis on maximization of agricultural production and yield, including maximization of water supply through addition of aqueducts for channelling water from distant streams and springs; waterwheels and pumps for raising water to nearby fields; large underground cisterns and reservoirs for storing water, and drainage systems for managing runoff (Hughes 1975); maximization of land area available for agricultural production through removal of forests and draining of swamps (White 1970:146–172); maximization of yield through application of green manure, fertilizers, and rotation of crops (White 1970: 86–172); maximization of crop and stock yields through breeding and improved husbandry practices (White 1970: 173–331); and maximization of farm labour through increased use of slaves and hired personnel (White 1970: 332–383

These efforts to maximize food system outputs were intimately linked to the growth and spread of cities throughout the Roman world. Modelled to a great extent on urban designs developed by the Greeks, and linked by paved highways, cities became the political centres of the Roman economy, exerting a powerful influence on their agricultural hinterlands (Foss 2002).

To these changes in rural and urban landscapes introduced by the Romans must be added their devotion to law, order and discipline—their «unwavering adherence to the idea of a controlled life, subject not to this or that individual, but to a system embodying the principle of justice and fair dealing» (Hamilton 1993: 129–130). In the end, this ideal ended up favouring the settled farmer over the nomad; the strong over the weak; and the landowner over the farm hand.

As a part of their Great Tradition the Byzantines continued to a significant extent the emphasis on maximization introduced as part of the Roman Great Tradition, but with modifications attributable in great measure to the rise of Byzantine Christianity, centred in Constantinople. Core components of their food system included continuation, and in certain locations, expansion of Roman system for maximizing water supply (Evenari, Shanan and Tadmor 1971; Patrich 1995: 483; Reifenberg 1955); addition of monasteries and estate farms as centres of agricultural production and distribution (Foss 2002: 95); intensification of cash crop production of olives and grapes (Foss 2002:92); and increased hierarchical organization of production due to increased concentration of political power in the hands of bishops at the expense of city endowments and private citizens (Foss 2002:71).

As in the case of the Roman Great Tradition, that of the Byzantines was essential to life in towns and cities. And every town, every city had its own church, or churches—often constructed of reused remains of destroyed Roman temples. Even the rural landscape took on a new character as monasteries and shrines were inserted in the midst of olive groves and along highways and paths linking cities and towns (Foss 2002:74).

Lessons for Today

In the foregoing pages I have attempted to highlight ways in which local level water management—as opposed to centralized control of water--has played a role in the development of various pristine (Mesopotamia and Egypt) and secondary (Levant) civilizations in the Ancient Near East. I have sought to show that the progress of various civilizations in the ANE has depended as much, and perhaps even more, on local level control of water as it has on state level control. This is because local level systems are far more resilient and thus less vulnerable to exhaustion and collapse—thus providing civilizations with a solid sub stratum on top of which successive dynasties and associated state level projects can rise and fall.

There are several important lessons for today that can be drawn from this study. The first is that local level water management strategies more often than not are so ordinary, so commonplace, that they tend to be ignored—taken for granted—by both ancient and modern observers. By contrast, large-scale water works, such as aqueducts and canals, are imposing—grand to see and behold as they criss-cross the rural landscapes of antiquity. No wonder, then, that scholarly research on ancient water management practices has tended to emphasize large-scale systems.

Elsewhere (2005) I have argued that in order to adequately analyze the rural landscapes of antiquity a three-pronged approach is needed that includes three interrelated perspectives—food systems, political economy and civilizations. Research on food systems investigates how the inhabitants of a given region or site interact with their local environment in order to obtain food, water, shelter and protection. This is the perspective that is most likely to bring little traditions—small-scale solutions--into view. The political economy perspective studies the ways in which local economic activities are connected to larger systems represented by market dominant elites in nearby towns or cities and by bureaucracies under the control of empires far beyond the local region. This perspective brings to light the role of the state in orchestrating local practices. The civilizational perspective expands the inquiry to examine underlying connections between various civilizations and the cultural and political projects of states and empires as they manifest themselves archaeologically in local regions. All three perspectives are needed in order to adequately study both small and large-scale water management systems in antiquity as well as today.

A second lesson—one that follows from this first—is that local level solutions more often than not tend to be undervalued and at times are deliberately discouraged by state-level bureaucracies. Being local—they can and usually do operate without the state—thus in a sense undermining the central project of all states—to create allegiance among constituent populations through rendering services that foster dependence. No wonder little is recorded about the little traditions for managing water in Egypt, for there was not much that the state could take credit for in this domain. To the extent that records pertaining to water management practices do exist in Mesopotamia, it is usually from places and periods when the state succeeded in capturing some degree of control over these systems. In the case of the Levant, practically nothing is preserved in written records of little traditions for managing rain water—archaeological excavations and surveys are the main—and almost exclusive--means of knowledge about such systems in the past in this region.

A third lesson has to do with the interplay of expert versus indigenous knowledge. To the extent that small-scale water systems are locally controlled, they are sustained by little traditions or indigenous knowledge. I define *indigenous knowledge* as «a bundle of intangible assets--including beliefs, sentiments, practical information and know-how—accumulated through centuries of experience and passed on from generation to generation within local communities as a means to cope with present and future challenges. Such knowledge stands in contrast to *expert knowledge*, by which I mean universalized systems of understanding and practice to which individuals gain access and proficiency through formal education or apprenticeship with an acknowledged master.

Since expert knowledge is normally required by states to build and maintain large-scale infra-structure systems such as paved roads, aqueducts and huge dams, a presumption tends to take hold within state bureaucracies that expert knowledge is automatically to be preferred over local or indigenous knowledge. This presumption, and associated sentiments about the inferiority of local knowledge, can and often does lead to policies and practices on the part of the state that ultimately undermine traditional practices. An example of this is the introduction of deep drilling, mechanical pumping stations, and water pipes throughout Jordan during the seventies and eighties in Jordan. This state-sponsored infrastructure initiative had the very likely unintended consequence of directly undermining centuries and millennia of local level—household-- reliance on cisterns and related rainwater capture and storage technologies. I have reported on this situation elsewhere and have recently become active in seeking to restore such little traditions in Jordan (see www.rainkeep.org).

At this writing I remain uncertain as to weather grass-roots efforts at restoring local level water control—such as Project Rainkeep—can truly succeed. What has been extinguished by the modern capitalist great tradition—and attendant consumer attitudes and expert knowledge—is not only an ancient technology, but a bundle of conservation-friendly attitudes and sentiments without which the restored technology alone will not be sufficient. The question is: what will it take to restore the *complex whole* of attitudes, sentiments, skills and practices that it takes for little traditions to live again.

Bibliography

Adams, Robert. Mc C. *Heartland of Cities: Surveys of Ancient Settlement and Land Use on the Central Floodplain of the Euphrates.* Chicago: University of Chicago Press, 1981.

_____. *Land Behind Baghdad: A History of Settlement on the Diyala Plains.* Chicago: University of Chicago Press, 1965.

Baer, Klaus. «Land and Water In Ancient Egypt.» Paper presented at the 28th International Congress of Orientalists, January 1971.

Bodley, John. *Cultural Anthropology: Tribes, States, and the Global System.* 3rd ed. Mountain View, CA: Mayfield Publishing Co., 2000.

Bowman, Alan K. *Egypt After the Pharaohs: 332 BC-AD 642 from Alexander to the Arab Conquest.* London: British Museum Publications, 1986.

Butzer, Karl. *Early Hydraulic Civilization in Egypt: A Study of Cultural Ecology.* Chicago: University of Chicago Press, 1976.

_____. « Environmental Archaeology.» In *The Oxford Encyclopedia of Archaeology in the Near East.* vol. 2. Ed.Eric M. Meyers. New York: Oxford University Pres, 1997: 244–252.

_____. «Irrigation.» In *The Oxford Encyclopedia of Ancient Egypt.* vol. 2. Ed. Donald B. Redford. Oxford: Oxford University Pres, 2001: 183–188.

_____. «Environmental Change in the Near East and Human Impact on the Land.» In *Civilizations of the Ancient Near East.* vols. 1 and 2. Eds. Jack Sasson, John Baines, Gary Beckman, and Karen Rubinson. Peabody, MA: Hendrickson Publishers, Inc., 1995. 123–151.

Charles, M.P. «Irrigation in Lowland Mesopotamia.» In *Irrigation and Cultivation in Mesopotamia.* part 1 vol. 4. Cambridge: Sumerian Agriculture Group, 1988.

Evenari, Michael, Leslie Shanan, and Naphtali Tadmor. *The Negev: The Challenge of Desert.* Cambridge, Massachusetts: Harvard University Press, 1971.

Eyre, Christopher J. «The Agricultural Cycle, Farming, and Water Management in the Ancient Near East.» In *Civilizations of the Ancient Near East.* vols. 3 and 4. Eds. Jack Sasson, John Baines, Gary Beckman, and Karen Rubinson. Peabody, MA: Hendrickson Publishers, Inc., 1995. 175–189.

Fernea, Robert A. *Shayhk and Effendi: Changing Patterns of Authority Among the El Shabana of Southern Iraq.* Cambridge, MA: Harvard University Press, 1970.

Foss, Clive. «Life in City and Country.» In *The Oxford History of Byzantium.* Oxford: Oxford University Press, 2002. 71–95.

Gasche, H. «Le Systeme Paleo-Fluviatile Au Sud-Ouest De Baghdad.» In *Irrigation and Cultivation in Mesopotamia.* Bulletin on Sumerian Agriculture. vol. 4. Cambridge: Aris & Phillips Ltd., 1988: 41–48.

Hamilton, Edith. *The Greek Way.* New York: W.W. Norton & Company, 1993.

Hansen, Donald P. «Samarra.» In *The Oxford Encyclopedia of Archaeology in the Near East.* vol. 4. Eds. Eric M. Meyers. New York: Oxford University Press, 1997. 472–473.

Hole, Arnold Frank. «Assessing the Past Through Anthropological Archaeology.» In *Civilizations of the Ancient Near East.* vols. 3 and 4. Eds. Jack Sasson, John Baines,

Gary Beckman, and Karen Rubinson. Peabody, MA: Hendrickson Publishers, Inc., 1995. 2715–2727.

_____. «Deh Luran.» In *The Oxford Encyclopedia of Archaeology in the Near East*. vol. 4. Eds. Eric M. Meyers. New York: Oxford University Press, 1997. 134–137.

Hughes, J. Donald. *Ecology in Ancient Civilizations*. Albuquerque, NM: University of New Mexico Press, 1975.

Iliffe, John. *Africans: The History of a continent*. Cambridge: Cambridge University Press, 1995.

LaBianca, Øystein. «Food Systems, Political Economy and Civilizations: A Framework for Investigating Historical Landscapes and Archaeological Tells in the Ancient Near East.» Paper presented at BASOR (Nov. 2004). Andrews University Institute of Archaeology.

_____.»Project Rainkeep.» On the web at http://www.rainkeep.org, 2004.

Libbey, William and Hoskins, Franklin E. *The Jordan Valley and Petra*. New York: G.P. Putnam's Sons, 1905.

Lukens-Bull, Ronald A. «Between Text and Practice: Considerations in the Anthropological Study of Islam.» In *Marburg Journal of Religion* Dec. 1999, 4:2.

Kramer, Samuel Noah. *The Sumerians: Their History, Culture, and Character*. Chicago: University of Chicago, 1963.

Marriott, McKim. «Little Communities in an Indigenous Civilization.» In *Village India: Studies in the Little Community*. Eds. McKim Marriot and Alan Beals. Chicago: University of Chicago Press, 1955.

Mendelssohn, K. *The Riddle of the Pyramids*. New York: Praeger, 1974.

Odner, Knut. *Tradition and Transmission: Bantu, Indo-European, and Circumpolar Great Traditions*. Bergen, Norway: Norse Publications. Bergen Studies in Social Anthropology No. 54, 2000.

Patrich, Joseph. «Church, State and the Transformation of Palestine – The Byzantine Period (324–640 CE).» In *The Archaeology of Society in the Holy Land*. London: Leicester University Press, 1995: 470–487.

Redfield, Robert. «Social Organization of Tradition.» In *Social Organization of Tradition* Nov. 1955 15:1: 13–21.

_____. *Human Nature and the Study of Society*. Chicago: University of Chicago Press, 1962.

Reifenberg, A. *The Struggle Between the Desert and the Sown: Rise and Fall of Agriculture in the Levant*. Jerusalem: Government Press, 1955.

Robins, Gay. «Mathematics, Astronomy, and Calendars in Pharaonic Egypt.» In *Civilizations of the Ancient Near East*. vol. 3 and 4. Ed. Jack M. Sasson. Peabody, Massachusetts: Hendrickson Publishers, Inc., 1995.

Saggs, H.W.F. *The greatness that was Babylon: a survey of the ancient civilization of the Tigris-Euphrates Valley*. London: Sidgwick & Jackson, 1988.

Steinkeller, P. «Notes on the Irrigation System in Third Millennium Southern Babylonia.» In *Irrigation and Cultivation in Mesopotamia*. Bulletin on Sumerian Agriculture. vol. 4. Cambridge: Aris & Phillips Ltd., 1988: 73–92.

Tubb, Jonathan N. *Canaanites*. Norman, OK: University of Oklahoma Press, 1998.

von Grunebaum, Gustave E. *Unity and Variety in Muslim Civilization*. Chicago: University of Chicago Press, 1955.

Wetterstrom, Wilma and Murry, Mary Anne. «Agriculture.» In *The Oxford Encyclopedia of Ancient Egypt*. vol. 1. Oxford: Oxford University Press, 2001: 37–44, 2001.

White, K.D. *Roman Farming*. Ithaca, New York: Cornell University Press, 1970.

Wittfogel, Karl. *Oriental despotism: A comparative study of total power*. New Haven: Yale University Press, 1957.

Woolley, C. Leonard. *The Sumerians*. New York: W.W. Norton & Company, 1965.

Presentation of authors

Silvia Álvarez is Professor of anthropology at the Department of Anthropology, Universidad Autónoma de Barcelona, Spain

Claudia Gonzalez Andricaín is a PhD student at the Department of Anthropology, La Universidad Autónoma de Barcelona, Spain

Frode F. Jacobsen is an Associate Professor of Anthropology and Health sciences at the Department of Public Health and Primary Health Care, University of Bergen, Norway

Øystein La Bianca is Professor of Archaeology and Anthropology at the Behavioral Science Faculty, Andrews University, Michigan, USA

Nina Laurie is Professor of Development and the Environmental Studies at the Department of Geography, University of Newcastle, England

Jorge Marcos is Professor of Archaeology and Anthropology at the Escuela Superior Politécnica del Litoral (ESPOL), Guayaquil, Ecuador

John-Andrew McNeish is a Senior Researcher at Christien Michelsen's Institute (CMI). Bergen, Norway

Franck Poupeau is a Post-doctoral fellow in Sociology at the Institut français d'études andines (IFEA) in Bolivia, and editor of the review Actes de la recherché en sciences socials, created by Pierre Bourdieu in 1975.

Pablo Regalsky is a PhD student in anthropology at the Department of Geography, University of Newcastle and Director of the Centro de Comunicación Social y Desarrollo Andino (CENDA), Bolivia.